The Changing Pros Communication ... Health, Psychosocial Adjustment, Academic Performance And Parent-Child Relationships

By :Bhatt, Sonia

CONTENTS

CHAPTER-1
INTRODUCTION

Today we are living in a revolutionary world of dots and coms and, within seconds, several new inventions are happening around the globe, media technology being one of them. Media technology has changed our lives giving us the freedom to perform activities from the comfort zone of our homes. The evolving technology has a strong impact on an individual's life especially teenagers as they are vulnerable to change. The invention of the cell phone, appearance of computers, laptops, and Internet communication has become a vital link in communicating with others. It has become inseparable part of our life and it is everywhere and it is impossible to escape from them. Twenty first century is the world of technology and Internet has grown leaps and bounds from the time of its origin to the present times globally.

There are **4.1 billion Internet users** in the world as at December 2018. This is compared to 3.9 billion Internet users in mid 2018 and about 3.7 billion Internet users in late 2017.According toInternet Statistics (2019) **Asia has the most Internet users of all continents** accounting for 49 per cent of all Internet users (down from about 50 percent in 2017 and up from about 48 per cent mid 2018). Europe is a runner up with 16.8 per cent of all Internet users.**China has the most Internet users of all country.** At over 802 million Internet users at the time of writing this, China currently accounts for almost 20 per cent of Internet users worldwide. It is trailed by India, with over 500 million Internet users.**The number of people using the Internet in China is more than double the population of the U.S.** and more than the combined population of the U.S., Japan, Russia, and Mexico. **98 per cent of Internet users in China are mobile.**

Iceland is the country with the highest Internet penetration in the world with an impressive 100 per cent of its citizens using the Internet.The Internet influenced retail sales to the tune of $2.84 trillion in 2018 and is expected to influence retail sales to the tune of $3.45 trillion in 2019. With a $205 billion Internet ad spend compared to a TV ad spend of $192 billion, global Internet advertising spend exceeded TV advertising spend for the very first time in 2017.An estimated 1.92 billion people are expected to purchase something online in 2019. 80 per cent of

Internet users in the U.S. are expected to make a purchase online in 2019 (Internet Statistics, 2019). Over 4 million blog posts are published on the Internet every day, over 500 million tweets are sent every day and over 5 billion Google searches are made every day.There are 342 million registered domain names as at the third quarter of 2018.Domain name registrations have grown by 3.5 per cent year over year. About 43.59 per cent of all domain names use the leading .com domain name extension.

Along with new technologies, the Internet has reshaped and improved many aspects of our lives by being integrated in our daily experiences. Internet has become more available, offers more services and its usage is growing in every age group. Approximately 46 per cent of the world population is on the Internet today, an incredible growth compared to only less than 1 per cent in 1995 (Internet Live Stats, 2017).

Established only a few decades ago, the Internet is a system of enormous technical and social complexity. It comprises a gigantic but almost invisible universe that inclined thousands of networks, millions of computers and billions of users across the world (Greenfield and Yan, 2006). It has linked about 190 countries for exchange of data, news and opinions. About 40 per cent of world's population is estimated to be the user of Internet. Largest numbers are from countries like China, America and India. In this modern era, Internet has become need of every bit of life. It has changed the way of living of human beings and has transformed old era of less access and facilities to a fully accessed and luxurious one. It has enclosed whole world in a box in which everything is easily accessible.

According to Kantar IMRB, a market research agency (2019) reportthe number of Internet users in India had registered an annual 18 per cent growth, and was estimated at 566 million as of December 2018, which was about 40 per cent of the overall Internet penetration, according to the study. The report also projected double-digit growth for 2019 and estimated that the number of Internet users will reach 627 million by the end of 2019. The total user base, 87 per cent, or 493 million Indians, were defined as regular users. About 293 million active Internet users reside in urban India, while there were 200 million active users in rural India. Moreover, 97 per cent of the users' accessed Internet using mobile phones. Increased availability of bandwidth, cost effective data plans, and increased awareness driven by government programmes seem to have rapidly bridged the digital gap between urban and rural India. Consequently, the penetration in rural India had increased from 9 per cent in 2015 to 25 per cent in 2018. Bihar registered the highest growth in Internet users across both urban and rural areas, registering a growth of 35 per cent over last year. The report also noted that the Internet usage is more gender balanced than ever before with women comprising 42 per cent of total Internet users. It is fascinating to note that the digital revolution is now sweeping small towns and villages perhaps driven by increased accessibility at affordable data costs. There is an increase in the usage of digital technology in rural India, as well where more than two-thirds of active Internet users are now accessing the Internet daily to meet their entertainment and communication needs.

Internet has limitless advantages in our daily life. Its advantages start with Google or other search engines which enable us to search any kind of information. Information, news or pictures, of the whole world can be easily accessed. Today no student, who has access to Internet, is left behind due to lack of study material or guidance. Internet is a source of enormous information. Scholars and researchers deliver their lectures sitting across the world through video conference. All these things have made Internet a boon in the field of education.

Internet is playing a major role in integrating or exchanging different cultures of the world. It has enabled us to reach out and know any culturein any part of the world. Internet is used by governments of many countries as a medium to promote their culture. Information about heritages or wonders of the world is easily available on the Internet.

Social networking is the one of the biggest achievements of Internet. The social networking sites like Facebook, Yahoo etc. have made this whole world like a family. Hence, these sites have strengthened the bond that people share amongst themselves around the globe.

Internet has enabled people to make online payments of any sort. People can book tickets of any mode of transport just by a few clicks. Now there is no need to rush to banks for transferring money as Internet has made it possible to do so at home through online banking. Online shopping is another pillar which is getting hike these days. Internet is a huge source of entertainment as well. Movies, songs, and videos are also available on Internet.

Most importantly, Internet has created millions of jobs and, hence, curbed the problem of unemployment in the world to a great extent. Internet's achievements are phenomenal. It is like a shining star which has magical rays of information and those who are exposed to these rays experience a transformation in their lives. However, in addition to the phenomenal growth of the Internet and its use, there has been an increasing concern worldwide regarding the risks related with over-use of Internet (Buchholz, 2009), especially among the adolescents.

Adolescent all over the world are growing up in a world, where the Internet, cell phones, text messaging and other technology dominates the communication and it is an integral part of everyday life. Adolescents and young adults represent the most users of these different tools, and the main purpose of use is social interaction and interpersonal communication.Computer access and use among adolescents and other age brackets have grown exponentially over the past decade. More than 80 per cent of American youth, aged 12 to 17, use the Internet, and nearly half log on every day (Lenhart, Madden, & Hitlin, 2005).

Although little research has been conducted on the effects of the Internet on various aspects of human development, the role of computers and the Internet as a means for socialization, education, information access, entertainment, shopping, and communication is increasing dramatically. Many adolescents reportedly prefer being online to other media, including the telephone, TV, and radio. Given that so many adolescents are spending so much time on the Internet, it is essential to be aware of its impact on adolescent behaviour, well-being, and development.

Adolescence is considered as the most difficult phase of life and as a result adolescents are not able to manage everything by their own and, thus become the victims of stress, anxiety and loneliness. Due to many reasons such as family problems, dissatisfaction with life, failure, prejudices, etc. adolescents feel lonely and alienated from the world. They start believing that happiness is available on the Internet and they search it in a virtual world. Social Networking Sites (SNS) grab attention, concentration and focus of the students and diverts them towards non-educational, unethical and inappropriate actions such as online chatting, random searching on the net and not focusing on their academics (Kuppuswamy & Shankar, 2011; Jung, 2012; Rosen, Cheever & Carrier, 2013). Excessive use of social media may lead adolescents towards anxiety and depression (Keeffe & Pearson, 2011). SNS have a negative impact on academic achievement as it decreases adolescents' concentration which results in distraction and poor academic performance (Barber, 1997; Survey Report of McCoy, 2013; Bhavana, 2014). Social media replaces the direct verbal face to face communication, thus, adolescents may lose their ability to learn and develop real human communication which may result in social anxiety (Pierce, 2009; Erwin, Turk, Heimberg, Fresco & Hantula, 2014; Akram, Mahmud & Mahmood, 2015; Drago, 2015; Parvathy & Suchithra, 2015;Siddiqui & Singh, 2016). SNS exposes young generation to cyber-crimes, bullying, defaming an individual and anti-social activities which might be harmful to youth, their families as well as for society (Chowdhury & Saha, 2015; Parvathy & Suchithra, 2015).

SNS also have a negative effect on the mental and physical health of adolescents as they prefer to remain indoors and access these sites all the time (Gupta, Arora & Gupta, 2013; Parvathy & Suchithra, 2015). Social media such as Facebook, Whatsapp, Twitter, Instagram and other networks have come to dominate teenagers' spare time. They watch their friends having fun and posting selfies and the temptation to compare their own life to the perfectly depicted life that friends portray online. Clicking selfies has become a symbol of prestige, fun and self-expression. People often portray their adventurous side by uploading crazy selfies and it is the selfie craze that has led to heavy injuries and even deaths of those attempting to take an ultimate unique selfie.

Findings from the study by scholars from Carnegie Mellon University and Indraprastha Institute of Information, Delhi (Gowen, 2016) revealed that our country has had far more selfie-related deaths than any other country in the world in the last two years. Most common types of killfie/selfie involved people falling from buildings, mountains, cliffs or other extreme heights. The selfie obsession can also be attributed to a high increase in smart phone sales.

This obsession of virtual world recently gave rise to a new life threatening game known as Blue Whale game. The Blue Whale game challenge is a suicide game where the player is given various tasks by an administrator for period of 50 days ranging from tasks like travelling alone, waking up early to listen to the disturbing music they send, watching the horror movies they send, cutting themselves, isolating themselves, believing that there is no hope and life is worthless and finally committing suicide. Origin of the game is believed to be in Russia and caused first suicide in 2015. Its developer is Philipp Budeikin, a student of Psychology. Another game which is widely used across globe is Player Underground's Battle Ground (PUBG). The game was released back in March 2018. It may be the most popular mobile game in the world right now, but PUBG is finding itself constantly mired in demands that it be banned, because its user's seeming inability to put the game down and deal with other things like living a real life. India isn't the only place where PUBG has run in to trouble with China's Online Gaming Ethics Review Committee having reportedly banned the game in December 2018 (David, 2019).

Just when people thought there couldn't be any more social media apps for young children to use, enter TikTok which is a free social media app designed for creating and sharing short music videos. TikTok is the most downloaded app on the App Store for its fifth consecutive quarter. However, its next quarter numbers may see a decline given that the app was banned in India temporarily this year, over pornographic and illegal content. The ban has been lifted recently. Millions of teenagers seeking their 15 seconds of fame are flocking to TikTok (Ucciferri, 2018).

The statistics are really shocking. Studies demonstrate that more frequent social network use is related to increased body dissatisfaction over a period of time among children. In an app where over 13 million videos are uploaded a day, it's impossible for parents to filter out all the inappropriate or dangerous content, without being accused of being a "helicopter parent".

Royal Society for Public Health (RSPH) and the Young Health Movement (YHM) (2017) conducted the study and found Instagram and Snapchat to be the most detrimental apps to mental health. It's not hard to see why since both platforms are image-focused; they are more likely to stir up feelings of inadequacy and anxiety in teens.

Hand in hand with this, the Internet has become a highly effective and profitable means of distributing sexually explicit material, as well as a sophisticated channel for compulsive sexual behavior, sex trafficking, and sex crimes (Galbreath & Berlin, 2002). According to a survey performed by the London School of Economics (2002), 90 per cent of children between ages 8 and 16 have viewed pornography on the Internet. In most cases, the sex sites were accessed unintentionally when a child, often in the process of doing homework, used an innocuous word to search for information or pictures. Such free access and exposure to this information by adolescents who have not yet developed a full maturity could pose negative impacts on adolescent development and could potentially manifest in their social interactions with peers, their sexual activity, and their emotional development (Subrahmanyam et al., 2006).

Internet addicts have characteristic features like emotional sensitiveness, maladaptation, inability to express themselves (Young and Rodgers, 1998; Calpan, 2005), lack of self-confidence (Bayraktar, 2001), academic and social problems (Niemz, 2005). Individuals who were dissatisfied or upset by a particular area or multiple areas of their lives had an increased likelihood of developing Internet addiction because they did not understand another way of coping (Young and Rodgers, 1997).

On one side the usage of Internet is increasing day by day and on the other hand many types of problems related to mental health are also increasing due to excessive usage of Internet. Among these problems stress, anxiety, maladjustment, depression and Internet addicted disorder, cyber sexual addiction and data smog are most common (Pandey, 2014). Kraut et al (2002) found that teenagers were most vulnerable to these negative effects. The increasing rate of adolescents suffering from some type of mental problems e.g. techno-stress, anxiety, maladjustment, depression, Internet addiction disorder and cyber sexual addiction has stirred parents, human resource managers, educationist, cyber psychologists, technologists and policy makers and has acquired an independent status.

Yachathoth, et al (2014) observed that excessive Internet use was evolving as a major negative consequence in adolescent and youth and they were at highest possible risk in terms of mounting problematic Internet use.

More and more people are getting engulfed in virtual world and drifting apart from their friends and family. Even children prefer to play online games rather than going out and mingling with other kids. This hampers a healthy social development in children (Nalwade,2102).

Many of the practicing Psychologists now opine that teenagers who are heavy users of social networking sites seem to be more depressed. They are reported to have interrupted sleep patterns. At times they miss schools and meals as well. The trend has gone to the extreme that Psychologists now have started asking for the online behavior of the patients of any sort before they do a full assessment (Varghese et al, 2013). Even continuous use of Internet and social networking has made the teens isolated from mainstream of the society and thereby decreased their curricular and cultural activities.

Due toeasy availability of Internet communication and excessive use of the technology people are more into virtual world and face to face communication with the families are getting affected andthe Internet attempts to substitute the human connection.

Social media is affecting parent- children relationship as well (Kaspersky, 2017). Relationships with family, friends and colleagues are changing as people communicate less face-to-face as a result of social media.

With connectivity so widespread, and tantalizing online activities constantly emerging, young people are spending more and more time online studying, learning, communicating, and entertaining themselves. That is certainly not a disorder, but for a small number it may be a slippery slope when combined with psychological and environmental variables that increase risk for addictive behavior. Similar to gambling, several online environments offer unique and compelling features that promote frequent use and can lead to signs of behavioral addiction. The variable ratio, partial reinforcement schedules programmed into slot machines maintain a very high and persistent response rate, and many online environments do the same thing. For instance, that kind of reward schedule is probably one reason young people check their smartphones so frequently for status updates or new text messages. 'Internet addiction disorder' may not be the right term, but the problems are very real and those students who are unable to control their online activities, whose grades drop and whose relationships with friends and family sour, definitely need help.

With each passing day, dependence on technology is increasing, as a result, the gap between the virtual and the real world is getting blurred. Social networking sites bring people together across the world in a larger sense but it creates social isolation in particular. Steps should be taken by teachers and parents to save adolescents from this situation by monitoring adolescents' social networking use and educating them about the potential hazards of social networking and reminding them that social networking sites are not an accurate representation of reality. The problems and disadvantages need to be fixed so that Internet transforms the world into more resourceful one.

Adolescents today are virtually at the crossroads, where they not only have to adapt effectively to the modernization of technology but also remain grounded to their traditional and cultural roots, which is of utmost importance in India. In such a scenario, the role of parents and teachers has increased manifold, as they have to enable them to learn and adapt to these changes but also, at the same time, ensure their optimal emotional, psychological and behavioural development. A distorted coping with technological advances can lead to delays and disturbances in the individuals' mental health, psychosocial adjustment, academic excellence and interpersonal relationships, and so can manifest in deviant behaviour or psychological issues. For healthy, physical and mental development of adolescents it is, therefore, of great importance that needs are satisfied and age specific developmental tasks are fulfilled.

Thus, under the current changing trends in technological advances, it is essential to study how adolescents indulge in Internet Communication. Moreover, it is also necessary to evaluate how their use of Internet communication affects their mental health, psychosocial adjustment, academic performance and their relationship with their mothers.

Keeping the above points in view the major intent of the present research work was:

1   To measure and compare Internet Communication (Internet Addiction, Internet Usage and Internet Attitude), mental health, psychosocial adjustment, academic performance and parent-child relationship among adolescent boys and girls.

2   To assess and compare the effect of Internet Communication(Internet Addiction, Internet Usage and Internet Attitude) on Mental Health of adolescents boys and girls.

3   To evaluate and compare the effect of Internet Communication(Internet Addiction, Internet Usage and Internet Attitude) on Psychosocial Adjustment of adolescents boys and girls.

4   To measure and compare the outcome of Internet Communication (Internet Addiction, Internet Usage and Internet Attitude) on Academic Performance of adolescent boys and girls.

5 To asses and compare the impact of Internet Communication(Internet Addiction, Internet Usage and Internet Attitude) on Parent-Child Relationship among adolescents boys and girls.

CHAPTER-2
THEORETICAL ORIENTATION

This chapter is organized into five sections. The first section deals with the Internet communication, history of Internet, its theories and how it leads to Internet addiction. The second section deals with the theoretical concept of mental health, its theories and factors influencing mental health. The third section covers the concept of psychosocial adjustment, its theories and factors related to psychosocial adjustment. The fourth section is followed by a conceptual discussion regarding academic performance. The last (fifth section) covers theoretical background of parent-child relationship, its theories and factors influencing Parent-child relationship.

2.1 INTERNET

The Internet, sometimes called simply "the Net", is a worldwide system of computer networks - a network of networks in which users at any one computer can, if they have permission, get information from any other computer (and sometimes talk directly to users at other computers).

In the early days, most people just used the Internet to search for information. Today's Internet is a constantly evolving tool that not only contains an amazing variety of information, but also provides new ways of accessing, interacting and connecting with people and content. As a result, new terms are constantly appearing as new technologies are introduced. Today, the Internet is a public, cooperative, and self-sustaining facility accessible to hundreds of millions of people worldwide.

The history of the Internet began with the development of electronic computers in the 1950s. The public was first introduced to the Internet when a message was sent over the ARPANetby Professor Leonard Kleinrock's laboratory at University of California, Los Angeles (UCLA). Packet switched networks such as ARPANET, Mark I at NPL in the UK, CYCLADES, Merit Network, Tymnet, and Telenet, were developed in the late 1960s and early 1970s using a variety of protocols. The ARPANET in particular led to the development of protocols for Internetworking, in which multiple separate networks could be joined together into a network of networks.

In 1982, the Internet protocol suite (TCP/IP) was standardized, and consequently, the concept of a world-wide network of interconnected TCP/IP networks, called the Internet, was introduced. Access to the ARPANET was expanded in 1981 when the National Science Foundation (NSF) developed the Computer Science Network (CSNET) and again in 1986 when NSFNET provided access to supercomputer sites in the United States from research and educational organizations. Commercial Internet service providers (ISPs) began to emerge in the late 1980s and early 1990s. The ARPANET was decommissioned in 1990. The Internet was commercialized in 1995 when NSFNET was decommissioned, removing the last restrictions on the use of the Internet to carry commercial traffic.

Since the mid-1990s, the Internet has had a revolutionary impact on culture and commerce, including the rise of near-instant communication by electronic mail, instant messaging, Voice over Internet Protocol(VoIP) "phone calls", two-way interactive video calls, and the World Wide Web with its discussion forums, blogs, social networking, and online shopping sites.

Today the Internet continues to grow, driven by ever greater amounts of online information, commerce, entertainment, and networking.

The history of the Internet in India began with the launch of the Educational Research Network (ERNET) in 1986.Machina (1995) the first publicly available Internet service in India was launched by state-owned Videsh Sanchar Nigam Limited (VSNL) in 1995. As of 31 December 2018, India had a population of 130 crore people (1.3 billion), 123 crore (1.23 billion) Aadhaar digital biometric identity cards, 121 crore (1.21 billion) mobile phones, 44.6 crore (446 million) smartphones, 56 crore (560 million) Internet users up from 481 million people (35 per cent of the country's total population) in December 2017, and 51 per cent growth in e-commerce. Government has embarked on the massive BharatNet, Digital India, Made in India and Startup India initiatives to expedite the Internet-based eco-system.

Digital India is a campaign launched by the government of India in 2015. It aims to make India a better-governed place of the world. This project has been approved by the prime minister of India, Sh. Narendra Modi and expected to be completed by the end of 2019. It is to facilitate Indian citizens with electronic government's services in order to reduce paperwork, improve work efficiency and save time. This plan will really ensure the growth and development in India especially in the rural areas by connecting rural regions and remote villages with high-speed Internet services. The overall project monitoring will be under the Prime Minister himself. Citizens of digital India may improve their knowledge and skill level after getting covered under the umbrella of Internet. It is an ambitious project which will benefit everyone especially villagers who travel long distance and waste time and money in doing paper works for various reasons. It is a most effective version (with nine pillars which are broadband highways, public Internet access programme, mobile connectivity everywhere, e-Kranti, e-Governance, information for all, IT for jobs, early harvest programmes and electronics manufacturing) of already existing National e-Governance Plan.

2.1.1 Internet Communication

Communication is the most popular use of the Internet, with email topping the list of all the technologies used. Other technologies, including video and audio conferencing and Internet telephony, are also available on the Internet. They require more multimedia capabilities of computer systems and are more taxing of network resources than the others.

Social media is the collection of online communication channels dedicated to community-based input, interaction, content-sharing and collaboration. Websites and applications dedicated to forums, micro, social networking, social bookmarking, social creation, and wikis are among the different types of social media.

Some prominent examples of social media are:

Facebook: Facebook is an American online social media and social networking service company which was launched in 2004, by Mark Zuckerberg, and his colleagues. It is a popular free social networking website that allows registered users to create profiles, upload photos and video, send messages and keep in touch with friends, family and colleagues.

Twitter: Twitter was created in 2006 by Jack Dorsey. It is a free micro blogging service that allows registered members to broadcast short posts called tweets. Twitter members can broadcast tweets and follow other users' tweets by using multiple platforms and devices.

Google+: Google+ launched in 2011 is an Internet-based social network that is owned and operated by Google.Features included the ability to post photos and status updates to the stream or interest based communities, group different types of relationships (rather than simply "friends") into Circles, a multi-person instant messaging, text and video chat called hangouts, events, location tagging, and the ability to edit and upload photos to private cloud-based albums.

Wikipedia: Wikipedia began with its launch in 2001, two days after the domain was registered by Jimmy Wales and Larry Sanger. It is a free, open content online encyclopedia created through the collaborative effort of a community of users known as Wikipedians. Anyone registered on the site can create an article for publication; registration is not required to edit articles.

LinkedIn: The Company was launched in 2003 by Reid Hoffman and founding team members from PayPal and Socialnet.com It is a business and employment-oriented service that operates via websites and mobile apps. The goal of the site is to allow registered members to establish and document networks of people they know and trust professionally.

Pinterest: It is a social curation website launched in 2010, for sharing and categorizing images found online. Pinterest requires brief descriptions but the main focus of the site is visual. Clicking on an image takes an individual to its original source.

Instagram: Instagram is a photo and video-sharing social networking service owned by Facebook and was launched in 2010. Instagram is a free photo and video sharing app. People can upload photos or videos to the service and share them with their followers or with a select group of friends. They can also view, comment and like posts shared by their friends on Instagram. Anyone 13 and older can create an account by registering an email address and selecting a username.

WhatsApp Messenger WhatsApp was founded in 2009. It is a freeware and cross-platformmessaging and Voice over IP (VoIP) service owned by Facebook. Originally, users could only communicate with others individually or in groups of individual users, but in September 2017, WhatsApp announced a forthcoming business platform that will enable companies to provide customer service to users at scale.

Paytm: Paytm is an Indian e-commerce payment system and digital wallet company. It was founded by Vijay Shekhar Sharma in 2010. Paytm became India's first payment app to cross over 100 million app downloads. By 2018, it started allowing merchants to accept Paytm, UPI and Card payments directly into their bank accounts at 0 percent charge. It also launched the 'Paytm for Business' app, allowing merchants to track their payments and day-to-day settlements instantly. This led its merchant base to grow to more than 7 million by March 2018.

2.1.2Internet Communication Theories

2.2.1. aUses and Gratifications Theory (UGT)

Uses and Gratifications Theory (UGT) was developed by Katz, Blumler, and Gurevitch (1974).It is an approach to understanding why and how people actively seek out specific media to satisfy specific needs. Most of the theories on media explained about the effects media had on people. It is the theory which explains how people use media for their need and its gratification. In other words one can say this theory states what people do with media rather than what media does to people. This communication theory is positivistic in its approach, based in the socio-psychological communication tradition, and focuses on communication at the mass mediascale.UGT discusses how users deliberately choose media that will satisfy given needs and allow one to enhance knowledge, relaxation, social interactions/companionship, diversion, or escape.

2.2.1.bSocial Presence Theory

Short, Williams, and Christie (1976) originally developed the theory of social presence to explain the effect telecommunications media can have on communication. According to social presence theory, communication is effective if the communication medium has the appropriate social presence required for the level of interpersonal involvement required for a task. On a continuum of social presence, the face-to-face medium is considered to have the most social presence and written, text-based communication the least. It is assumed in social presence theory that in any interaction involving two parties, both parties are concerned both with acting out certain roles and with developing or maintaining some sort of personal relationship. These two aspects of any interaction are termed interparty and interpersonal exchanges (Short, Williams, & Christie, 1976). Computer Mediated Communication (CMC) researchers later used this theory to explain that was inherently impersonal because nonverbal and relational cues common in face-to-face communication are filtered out of CMC (Walther & Parks, 2002).

2.2.1.c Media Richness Theory (MRT)

Daft and Lengel (1986) developed a theory about organizational communication known as Media Richness Theory. Essentially, online text-based communication is said to be less rich than other media on a number of important levels. Media Richness Theory provides a framework for describing a communication medium's ability to reproduce the information sent over it without loss or distortion. For example, a phone call will not be able to reproduce visual social cues such as gestures. This makes it less rich (as a communication medium) than video conferencing, which is able to communicate gestures to some extent, but more rich than email. Specifically, MRT states that the more ambiguous and uncertain a task is, the richer format of media suits it. Other communication scholars have tested the theory in order to improve it, and more recently MRT has been retroactively adapted to include new media communication mediums, such as improved video and online conferencing.

2.2.1.d Group Theories

There are also a number of technology related theories that address how (media) technology affects group processes. Broadly, these theories are concerned with the social effects of media communication. Some (e.g., media richness) are concerned with questions of media choice (i.e., when to use what medium effectively).

In the late 1980s and early 1990s, researchers began to study the effects of Computer-Mediated Communication (CMC). Some concluded that CMC was inherently antisocial and impersonal (Walther, Anderson, & Park, 1994 and Walther, 1996). While Hiltz & Turoff (1993) acknowledged that interpersonal relationships might be fostered through CMC, early research suggested and convinced others that CMC was better at task-oriented communication (Walther& Parks, 2002). These early CMC researchers turned to social presence theory to make sense of their findings.

2.2.1.eTime, Interaction, and Performance Theory (TIP)

Time, Interaction, and Performance (TIP) theory was introduced by McGrath's (1991). Group work happens in every corner of our daily life like Community, Nation, Military, Job, Family, Marriage, Friendships etc. We can't exist without working in a group, thus one's existence and development in life are based on group work. McGrath's Time, Interaction, and Performance (TIP) theory was adopted for theoretical analysis framework. TIP theory suggests that group members contribute to the group according to three team functions: (1) production completion of the task, (2) group well-being maintenance of group relationships, and (3) members support individual group member role or relationship within the group. TIP theory also suggests that regardless of the function, group members contribute to the group at one of four modes of activity when working on a project. These activities represent phases of the completion of a task and include (1) inception, (2) problem solving, (3) conflict resolution, and (4) execution. This model also states that groups adopt these four modes with respect to each of three team functions: production, well-being and member support. In this sense, groups are seen as "always acting in one of the four modes with respect to each of the three functions, but they are not necessarily engaged in the same mode for all functions, nor are they necessarily engaged in the same mode for a given function on different projects that may be concurrent".

2.2.1.fThe Social Identity model of De individuation Effects (SIDE)

The SIDE theory was developed and first named in 1991 by Lea and Spears, and then later expanded on in 1992. This theory is important in understanding computer mediated technology and communication.The SIDE model expands on the basic de individuation theory that examines how in crowds people will act in ways that are often not perceived as rational. When somebody is in a crowd there is a certain amount of anonymity that can affect how they will act. For example, normally if a rational person did not agree with a controversial decision made by a company, they would not usually go up to the company's building by themselves and throw a glass bottle at it. On the other hand if a person is in a crowd of one hundred people and everyone is throwing glass bottles, then the person may be inclined to act in an irrational way and proceed to deface the building with glass bottles. The SIDE model distinguishes cognitive and strategic effects of a communication technology. Cognitive effects occur when communication technologies make "salient" particular aspects of personal or social identity. SIDE, therefore, sees the social and the technological aspect as mutually determining, and the behavior associated with particular communication forms as the product or interaction of the two.

2.2.1.gSocial Information Processing Theory (SIP)

Social Information Processing theory, also known as SIP, is an interpersonal communication theory which was developed by Walther (1992). Social Information Processing theory explains how people interact with other people online without nonverbal cues and develop and manage relationships in a computer-mediated environment. While the term has traditionally referred to those communications that occur via computer-mediated formats (e.g., instant messages, e-mails, chat rooms), it has also been applied to other forms of text-based interaction such as text messaging. In computer-mediated environments, interpersonal relationship development may require more time to develop than traditional face-to-face (FtF) relationships. Social information processing theory argues that online interpersonal relationships may demonstrate the same relational dimensions and qualities as FtF relationships. These online relationships may help facilitate interactions that would not have occurred face-to-face due to factors such as geography and intergroup anxiety.

2.2.1.hSignalling Theory, Warranting Theory and Identity Development

The process of creating profiles has been a major focus of theoretical and empirical discussion. The common features of profiles include personal information such as one's name, location, school affiliation, occupation, and personal interests such as favourite movies or music. Other vital components of the profile are pictures, videos, and the comments one's peers leave on the page. Profiles can be updated at any time and some sites like MySpace allow individuals control as to how their profile looks. Using programming techniques, youth frequently apply "skins" to their MySpace profiles that completely alter the visual design or interface of their pages (Boyd, 2008).

Signalling theory is one framework used to understand how individuals disclose information on their Social Networking Services (SNS) profiles. Donath (2007) observes that, "Whether face-to-face or online, much of what people want to know is not directly observable".

Signalling theory examines how one's self-presentation in Social Networking Services develops identity and trust with others. For example, when a user displays a contact as a "friend" he or she is in an indirect way vetting that that person is in fact who they claim to be. Thus, members who indiscriminately add any and all friend requests (including fake profiles or people they do not know) in an effort to seem popular may instead damage their credibility and trustworthiness to others. Among teenagers, Boyd (2008) finds that "it is cool to have Friends on MySpace but if you have too many Friends, you are seen as a MySpace whore".

In a similar vein, warranting theory suggests that human beings do in fact judge others based on cues in SNS profiles. Walther and colleagues (2008) have shown that an individual (on Facebook) is consistently rated as physically and socially attractive when his or her friends are also attractive (Walther, Van Der Heide, Kim, Westerman & Tong, 2008). Positive and negative comments left on a person's Facebook wall also greatly influence whether they are seen as attractive. In addition to judging others based on their profiles, SNS users appear to judge the credibility of profile information quite consistently. On SNS we are judged by the company we keep.

2.1.3 Advantages of Internet

Internet provides a wide range of benefits and some of them are as follows:

Advancement of communication

The target of the Internet has always been communication. The Internet has excelled beyondthe expectation. Our earth has become a global village due to its introduction. Now we can establish global friendship to explore in a fraction of second.

Availability of Information 24/7

The Internet provides a vital source of information non-stop 24/7. We have search engines like Google, Bing, and Yahoo where we can find about every subject like government law and service, financial matters, economic affairs, market information, educational and academic issues, new ideas and technical support.

Global Audience

The Internet has a huge number of audiences throughout the world. If a person wants to advertise his/her product or something else it is very easy to reach a wider range of audience.

Online Money Transfer

Money transfer through the Internet system is very popular now and this is very safe. This is problems free than any other money transfer system. People can transfer money worldwide very quickly.

Provide Entertainment

Entertainment is another popular reason for which people prefer Internet. Games, movies, music, and chatting are available through the Internet and people love to surf it for fun and amusement.

Social Networking

Now a day's social networking is the vast popular thing among every class of people. Social networking sites like Facebook, Twitter or Google Plus plays a vital role in the exchange of ideas among people. In fact, social networking can play a massive role in business, social activities, even politics.

Access to Services

Many services are now provided on the Internet such as online banking, job searching, purchasing and booking tickets, hotel reservation guidance and tips service. Internet allows services at cheap rate overcoming time and distance barriers.

Basis for E-commerce

Buying and selling on the Internet is known as electronic commerce or E-commerce. Every single product and service can be available at our doorsteps because of E-commerce and this is possible across the globe via the Internet.

Undoubtedly Internet has a great impact in every aspect of life, but every action has an opposite reactions as well. There are some disadvantages of Internet as well that are mentioned below:

2.1.4 Disadvantages of Internet

It's easy accessibility poses greater risks and dangers for youth as compared to other forms of media. According to the National Altitudinal Poll (2006) the number one media concern for parents has shifted from television to the Internet. 85 per cent of parents reported that among all forms of media, the Internet posed the greatest risk to their children (Common Sense Media, 2006). Parental concerns are valid, especially considering that teens are essentially free to view and post whatever they choose and communicate with whomever they want. On one side social networking sites are integrating the world but, on other hand it has become a medium for dividing the world. Some forces are using these sites for promoting hatred for other religions, castes etc. Terrorist groups are also using it to distract youth from mainstream life and engaging them in militant activities. Also pornography has been proven curse for our society and culture. It has become a worldwide business and has played a significant role in increasing crimes against women. It has also created fear among female Internet users.

Although the Internet has consistent positive impacts on modern society, it has also caused various societal concerns about privacy, security, pornography and Internet crime (Greenfield & Yan, 2006).

Theft of Personal Information

The most significant threat of Internet is hacking. Hacking is a disadvantage that has created a sense of insecurity among Internet users. Online money transfer has also become little insecure due to hacking. People can hack and steal personal information like name, address, credit card number, etc. which brings financial loss to a person. It is most significant threat of Internet. A hacker can steal anyone's personal document, picture, video or anything which one can store in one's computer and sometimes it can get bigger.

Spamming

It refers to sending of huge unwanted e-mails intentionally to destroy the computer systems. Such activity is harassment to the computer user.

Virus Threat

Virus is a program which damages the functioning of computer systems. It comes through Internet and can crash the total system on the sly.

Pornography

There are thousands of pornographic sites on the Internet which can adversely affect an individual.

Wrong Information

Though everyone can run website and there are many free blogging platform and document sharing site on the Internet. As a result there is a lot of information which is floating on the Internet which is not authentic or relevant. It is one of the most important disadvantages of Internet.

2.1.5Internet Addiction

Internet addiction is typically described as a state where an individual has lost control of the Internet use and keeps using Internet excessively to the point where he/she experiences problematic outcomes that negatively affects his/her life (Young & Abreu, 2011). Examples of such outcomes are cases where individuals lost sleep or skipped meals because they were spending excessive time on the Internet, or where Internet use has resulted in conflicts with family members or led to the detriment of a job or educational career.

Internet Addiction Disorder (IAD), a psycho-physiological disorder involving tolerance; withdrawal symptoms; affective disturbances; and interruption of social relationships, is beginning to become a problem in today's society. The Internet is becoming less fun and more harmful. It is now more commonly called Problematic Internet Use (PIU), Compulsive Internet Use (CIU), Internet overuse, problematic computer use, pathological computer use. A disorder which refers to excessive computer use with the consequences of interfering and disrupting daily life.

IAD was originally proposed as a disorder in a satiricalhoax by Ivan Goldberg (1995). He took pathological gambling, as diagnosed by the Diagnostic and Statistical Manual of Mental Disorders (DSM-V, 2013), as his model for the description of IAD. The possible future classification of IAD as a psychological disorder continues to be debated and researched in the psychiatric community. A systematic review of Pathological Internet Use (PIU) literature identified the lack of standardization in the concept as a major impediment to advancing this area of study. Other habits such as reading, playing computer games, or watching very large numbers of Internet videos, such as those on YouTube, are troubling only to the extent that these activities interfere with normal life. IAD is often divided into subtypes by activity, such as gaming; online social networking; blogging; email; excessive, overwhelming, or inappropriate pornography use; or Internet shopping (shopping addiction). Thomson (2016) suggested that prevalence of Internet addiction varies considerably among countries and is inversely related to quality of life.

Griffiths'(2005) six criteria of Internet addiction are:

Salience: When the use of the Internet becomes the most important activity in an individual's life and dominates their thinking, feelings and behavior. It can lead to cognitive distortions, irrational cravings and deterioration of socialized behavior For example, even when the people are "off line," they are thinking about the next time they will be on line.

Mood Modification: People report a positive subjective experiences which people report as a consequence of engaging in Internet use and which can be seen as a coping strategy for them (i.e. they experience an arousing "buzz" or a "high," or they experience a tranquilizing feeling of "escape" or "numbing").

Tolerance: The process by which users increase the level of Internet use they partake in, to achieve its mood-modification effects. There is a tendency to gradually increase the amount of time spent on line, in order to expand or extend those effects.

Withdrawal Symptoms: The unpleasant feeling-states and/or physical effects which occur when Internet use is discontinued or suddenly reduced. Withdrawal symptoms might include like shakiness, moodiness, or irritability.

Conflict: The various conflicts emerging as a result of the person's excessive Internet use are interpersonal conflict; conflicts with other activities (e.g., job, social life, other interests); or conflicts within the individual (intra psychic conflict and/or feelings of loss of control).

Relapse: The tendency for repeated reversals to, or recurrence of prior behavioral patterns. Even the most extreme patterns of excessive Internet use or addiction can be rapidly restored by the user – even after periods of abstinence or control.

2.2 MENTAL HEALTH

The word "health" refers to a state of complete emotional and physical well-being. Health is the ability of a biological system to acquire, convert, allocate, distribute, and utilize energy with maximum efficiency. Health is not just absence of disease but a state of overall wellbeing. In 1948, the World Health Organization (WHO) defined health with a phrase that is still used today. "Health is a state of complete physical, mental and social well-being and not merely the absence of disease or infirmity."

More recently, researchers have defined health as the ability of a body to adapt to new threats and infirmities. They base this on the idea that modern science has dramatically increased human awareness of diseases and how they work in the last few decades. Mental and physical health is the two most commonly discussed types of health. People also talk about "spiritual health," "emotional health," and "financial health," among others. These have also been linked to lower stress levels and enhance mental and physical wellbeing.

The idea of mental health is complex and comprehensive. This term consists of two words 'Mental' and 'Health'. Health generally means sound condition or well-being or freedom from diseases. It is mostly related to physical health of the individual. A person is said to be physically healthy when his body is functioning well and he is free from pains and troubles. Mental health is as important as physical health to an individual's holistic development. It refers to a person's, emotional, social and psychological well-being. Mental health has been mentioned as the ability of the person to balance one's desires and aspirations, to cope with the stresses of life and to make psychosocial adjustment. Mental health is a term used to describe how well the individual is adjusted to the demands and opportunities of life. Moreover, mental health is not only the absence of depression, anxiety, or any mental disorder. It is an individual's ability to enjoy life, bounce back after difficult experiences, achieve balance, adapt to adversity, feel safe and secure and achieve one's potential.

Mental health is a vital component of the total health of an individual because one's entire thought process and ideas takes place in mind, whicheventually guide, shape and regulate communication, and behavior and determine personal and social functioning as well as adjustment (Bhargava and Raina, 2007).

In Indian way, mental makeup constitutes three **gunas** or characteristics as **Sattav, Rajas** and **Tamas**.The imbalance of these gunas cause mental disorders. These gunas are in 'manas' (mind) since birth but a normal person has to maintain their equilibrium. Lord Krishna also stresses in Gita on three gunas to be kept in balance and mind is the key for this. The mental temperaments of human beings, known as gunas in Sanskrit, are of three types. Each has a distinct character of its own. They are known as: tamas or inactive, rajas or active and sattva or transactive. Tamas is the state of thoughts in inertia; a mood of lethargy, indolence, indifference. Indisposed to activity, in a condition of sloth and sleep and with no intellectual conviction to pursue, nor emotional feeling to manifest, a person steeped in tamas lives a dull, inactive life, with hardly any response to the world. Rajas is the state of passionate, desirous and agitated thoughts when a person bristles with frenzied actions leading to his involvement in the affairs of the world. Sattva is the state of thoughts in equanimity, serenity, objectivity when a person is poised, mature, contemplative, detached from worldly involvement and excitement. Hence, he is described as being trans-active. Sattva, rajas and tamas composed in different proportions account for the heterogeneous variety of human beings. Every individual possesses all three gunas (Srivastava 2012)

Mental health can, thus, be defined as the emotional, behavioral, and social maturity or normality; the absence of a mental or behavioral disorder; a state of psychological well-being in which one has achieved a satisfactory integration of one's instinctual drives acceptable to both oneself and one's social milieu; an appropriate balance of love, work, and leisure pursuits (Med Lexicon's Medical Dictionary, 2015).

2.2.1Theories of Mental Health

2.2.1.aPsychodynamic Theory

Freud developed the first psychodynamic theory, in the late 1800s called psychoanalytic theory. Psychodynamic theory states that events in our childhood have a great influence on our adult lives, and in shaping our personality. Events that occur in childhood can remain in the unconscious, and cause problems as adults. In essence, the child passes through different stages. Major conflicts or excessive gratification at any of the stages can lead to fixation,therefore,if an adult experiences great personal problems, he or she will tend to show regression (going back through the stages of the psychosexual development) to the stage at which he or she had previously been fixated. Thus, because conflicts cause anxiety, and the ego defends itself against anxiety by using several defence mechanisms to prevent traumatic thoughts and feelings reaching consciousness, mental disorders can arise when an individual has unresolved conflicts and traumas from childhood. Defence mechanisms may be used to reduce the anxiety caused by such unresolved conflicts, but they act more as sticking plaster than as a way of 'sorting out' an individual's problem. Freud proposed a psychological model in which behavior is explained in terms of past experiences and motivational forces. Actions are viewed as stemming from inherited instincts, biological drives, and attempts to resolve conflicts between personal needs and social requirements. His outstanding contribution to psychotherapy was his concept of psychoanalysis as the means to unlock the unconscious and resolve these childhood conflicts.

2.2.1.bBehavioral Theory

The behaviorist movement began in 1913 with John Watson. Behaviourism emphasizes the role of environmental factors in influencing behaviour, to the near exclusion of innate or inherited factors. This amounts essentially to a focus on learning. According to behavioral theory, a person's behavior is the result of learning that has occurred in response to a stimulus. Ivan Pavlov (1897) is credited with discovering the behavioral theory of classical conditioning. According to Behavioural Theory (Skinner, 1938, 1953, Pavlov, 1897) people learn new behaviors through classical or operant conditioning. Behavioral theory seeks to explain human behavior by analyzing the antecedents and consequences present in the individual's environment and the learned associations he or she has acquired through previous experience. Behavioral theories of depression emphasize the role maladaptive actions play in the onset and maintenance of depression. These theories stem from work concerning the principles of learning and conditioning from the early to mid-1900s. Ivan Pavlov and B. F. Skinner are often credited with the establishment of behavioral psychology with their research on classical conditioning and operant conditioning, respectively. Collectively, their research established that certain behaviors could be learned or unlearned, and these theories have been applied in a variety of contexts, including abnormal psychology. Theories specifically applied to depression emphasize the reactions individuals have to their environment and how they develop adaptive or maladaptive coping strategies.Behavioral theories also explain that learning can also occur through rewards and punishments. (Thorndike 1898; Watson 1913; and Skinner 1938). It's a scientific approach that limits the study of psychology to measurable or observable behavior.

2.2.1.cHumanistic Theory

Humanistic theory began as a movement against psychoanalysis and behaviorism in the 1950s and 1960s. It remains a viable "third force" in psychology, because it provides a unique perspective on mental health and psychopathology. This theory questions the medical model and the usefulness of the ever-increasing labeling of mental disorders. Instead, it emphasizes the study of the whole person, especially each person's potentials. It assumes that individuals have the freedom and courage to transcend biological and environmental influences to create their own future. Adopting a holistic approach, humanistic psychology emphasizes the phenomenological reality of the experiencing person in context. It describes both historical and current humanistic perspectives of mental health. It also indicates how deficiencies in meeting basic psychological human needs can result in psychopathology. Humanism is grounded in the belief that people are innately good. This type of psychology holds that morality, ethical values, and good intentions are the driving forces of behavior, while adverse social or psychological experiences can be attributed to deviations from natural tendencies.

2.2.1.dCognitive Theory

In the 1950's Albert Ellis, and Aaron Beck, independently developed two very similar theories which are referred to as cognitive behavioral theory. This theory proposes that depressed people think differently than non-depressed people, and it is this difference in thinking that causes them to become depressed. For example, depressed people tend to view themselves, their environment, and the future in a negative, pessimistic light. As a result, depressed people tend to misinterpret facts in negative ways and blame themselves for any misfortune that occurs. This negative thinking and judgment style functions as a negative bias and makes it easy for depressed people to see situations as being much worse than they really are. It consequently increases the risk that such people will develop depressive symptoms in response to stressful situations. According to Beck (1967), the way one interpret environmental events is a function of his/her core schema. A core schema is a central assumption about oneself, others, and the world. These assumptions influence one's feelings and behavior. Behavioral learning theory emphasizes the role of the environment, whereas, cognitive theory emphasizes the key role of the mind's cognitions in determining behavior. These cognitions include a person's thoughts, feelings, beliefs, and perceptions. Nonetheless, both Ellis (1956)and Beck (1967) sought to modify an individual's dysfunctional thoughts, in order to produce a change in emotions and behavior. Problems occur when distorted thinking patterns influence one's interpretation of environmental events.

2.2.1.eBiological Theory

Biological theory analyzes how the brain, neurotransmitters, and other aspects of our biology influence our behaviors, thoughts, and feelings. This field of psychology is often referred to by a variety of names including biopsychology, physiological psychology, behavioral neuroscience, and psychobiology. Bio psychologists often look at how biological processes interact with emotions, cognitions, and other mental processes and influence an individual's mental health (Wickens, 2005).

2.2.1.fMental Health Model

Mental Health Model (Veit and Ware, 1983), states that there are six components of mental Health, which are anxiety, depression, loss of behavior, general positive affect, life satisfaction and emotional ties.

Anxiety is an emotion characterized by an unpleasant state of inner turmoil, often accompanied by nervous behavior such as pacing back and forth, somatic complaints, and rumination. It is the subjectively unpleasant feelings of dread over anticipated events, such as the feeling of imminent death. Anxiety is not the same as fear, which is a response to a real or perceived immediate threat, whereas anxiety is the expectation of future threat. Anxiety is a feeling of uneasiness and worry, usually generalized and unfocused as an overreaction to a situation that is only subjectively seen as menacing. It is often accompanied by muscular tension, restlessness, fatigue and problems in concentration. Anxiety can be appropriate, but when experienced regularly the individual may suffer from an anxiety disorder.

Depression is a mood disorder characterized by persistently low mood and a feeling of sadness and loss of interest. Depression is a persistent problem, not a passing one. The average length of depressive episode is six to eight months. Depression is different from the fluctuations in mood that people experience as a part of normal life.Temporary emotional responses to the challenges of everyday life do not constitute depression. Likewise, even the feeling of grief resulting from the death of someone close is not itself depression if it does not persist.

Loss of Behavior reflects instability in controlling emotions, behavior, thoughts and feelings by an individual in any situation.

General Positive Affect refers to how much individuals enjoy their daily lives, even when confronted with problematic situations and they are able to be relaxed.

Life Satisfaction is the way in which people show their emotions and feelings (moods) and how they feel about their directions and options for the future. It is a measure of well-being and may be assessed in terms of mood, satisfaction with relations with others and with achieved goals, self-concepts, and self-perceived ability to cope with daily life. It is having a favourable attitude of one's life rather than an assessment of current feelings. Life satisfaction has been measured in relation to economic standing, amount of education, experiences, and residence, as well as many other topics. Life satisfaction is a key part of subjective wellbeing

Emotional Ties An emotional tie is the bond formed between people who have a connection with one another. Family members, friends, lovers, colleagues, acquaintances, etc. all form some type of emotional bond that acts like an elastic band as it stretches and relaxes due to our emotional thoughts and behaviors toward one another. Family members are bound by genetics and attachments formed which are based upon the time spent together or apart. A child whose parent has left him/her at a young age for a prolonged period of time may feel abandoned and the emotional tie eventually breaks. Friends form emotional ties through the discovery of common interests and activities. Colleagues bond as they work together to complete work or school assignments. Relationships are formed and emotional ties are balanced as people work through daily problems; spend time together, and how life events are experienced.

2.2.1.gSeligman's well-being Theory

Seligman (2011) proposed a theory of Psychological well-being and happiness comprising five salient elements, namely, positive emotion, engagement, positive relationships, meaning, and accomplishment. It is also known as PERMA model. Seligman believes that these five elements can help people reach a life of fulfilment, happiness, and meaning.

P – Positive Emotion: Being able to focus on positive emotions is more than just smiling; it is the ability to be optimistic and view the past, present, and future from a positive perspective. This positive view of life can help people in relationships, work, and inspire them to be more creative. There are also many health benefits to optimism and positivity.

E – Engagement: It is important for everyone to be able to find activities that need engagement. Engagement in the activities in one's life is important for him/her to learn, grow and nurture his/her personal happiness. Everyone is different and people find enjoyment in different things whether it's playing an instrument, playing a sport, dancing, working on an interesting project at work or even just pursuing it as a hobby.

R – Relationships: Social connections and relationships are one of the most important aspects of life. Humans are social animals that thrive on connection, love, intimacy, and a strong emotional and physical interaction with other humans. Building positive relationships with one's parents, siblings, peers, and friends are important to spread love and joy. Having strong relationships gives people support in difficult times.

M – Meaning: Having a purpose and meaning is important to living a life of happiness and fulfillment. Rather than the pursuit of pleasure and material wealth, there is an actual meaning to people's life. Such meaning gives people a reason and a purpose in life.

A – Accomplishments: Having goals and ambitions in life can help people to achieve things that can give them a sense of accomplishment. One should make realistic goals that can be met and just putting in the effort to achieving those goals can give people a sense of satisfaction. When they finally achieve those goals a sense of pride and fulfillment will be reached. Having accomplishments in life is important to push oneself to thrive and flourish.

2.2.2 FACTORS AFFECTING MENTAL HEALTH

Most mental health professionals believe that there are a variety of contributing factors to the onset of a mental illness. Studies have found that there are physical, social, environmental and psychological causes for mental illness (Bhandari 2018). It is becoming clear through research that many of these conditions are caused by a combination of biological, psychological, and environmental factors.

2.2.2.a Biological Factors

Some mental illnesses have been linked to an abnormal balance of special chemicals in the brain called neurotransmitters. Neurotransmitters help nerve cells in the brain to communicate with each other. If these chemicals are out of balance or are not working properly, messages may not make it through the brain correctly, leading to symptoms of mental illness. In addition, defects in or injury to certain areas of the brain have also been linked to some mental conditions.Other biological factors that may be involved in the development of mental illness include:

Genetics (Heredity): Many mental illnesses run in families, suggesting that people who have a family member with a mental illness are more susceptible to developing a mental illness. Susceptibility is passed on in families through genes. Experts believe many mental illnesses are linked to abnormalities in many genes, not just one. That is why a person inherits a susceptibility to a mental illness and doesn't necessarily develop the illness. Mental illness itself occurs from the interaction of multiple genes and other factors such as stress, abuse, or a traumatic event, which can influence, or trigger an illness in a person who has an inherited susceptibility to it.

Infections: Certain infections have been linked to brain damage and the development of mental illness or the worsening of its symptoms. For example, a condition known as Pediatric Autoimmune Neuropsychiatric Disorder (PANDA) associated with the Streptococcus bacteria has been linked to the development of obsessive-compulsive disorder and other mental illnesses in children.

Brain defects or injury: Defects in or injury to certain areas of the brain has also been linked to some mental illnesses.

Prenatal damage: Some evidence suggests that a disruption of early fetal brain development or trauma that occurs at the time of birth, for example, loss of oxygen to the brain, may be a factor in the development of certain conditions, such as autism.

Other factors: Poor nutrition and exposure to toxins, such as lead, may play a role in the development of mental disorders.

2.2.2.bPsychological Factors

Psychological, emotional, and physical trauma is the result of extraordinarily stressful events that shatter one's sense of security, making him/her feel helpless in a dangerous world.

Traumatic experiences often involve a threat to life but any situation that leaves people feeling overwhelmed can be traumatic, even if it doesn't involve physical harm. It's not the objective factor that determine whether an event is traumatic or not but one's subjective emotional experience(Canadian Mental Health Association, 2016). The more frightened and helpless he/she feels, the more likely he/she is to be traumatized. A traumatic event involves one's experience, or repeating events of being overwhelmed that can be precipitated in weeks, years, or even decades as the person struggles to cope with the immediate circumstances, eventually leading to serious, long-term negative consequences. Some psychological factors that contribute to mental health are:

Self-esteem

This is the value we place on ourselves, our positive self-image and sense of self-worth. People with high self-esteem generally have a positive outlook and are satisfied with themselves most of the time.

Feeling loved

Children, who feel loved, trusted and accepted by their parents and others are far more likely to have good mental health. They are also more likely to feel comfortable, safe and secure, and are better able to communicate and develop positive relationships with others.

Confidence

Youth should be encouraged to discover their own unique qualities and have the confidence to face challenges and take risks. Young people who are brought up to have confidence in themselves are more likely to have a positive attitude, and to lead happy and productive lives.

Family breakup or loss

Separation or divorce or the loss of a parent or sibling is extremely painful. Finding ways to cope and adjust to the changes brought by these events is critical for everyone, but particularly for youth. How grief is handled can affect young people negatively for years to come.

Difficult behavior

When people are unhappy, they either internalize their unhappiness or act out. The latter usually appears as bad or difficult behavior, such as using abusive language, being aggressive or violent, damaging property, stealing, lying, refusing to comply with requests or expectations at school or home, or displaying other inappropriate actions.

Physical ill health

Diseases, injuries and other physical problems often contribute to poor mental health and sometimes mental illness. Some physical causes (such as birth trauma, brain injury or drug abuse) can directly affect brain chemistry and contribute to mental illness. More commonly, poor physical health can affect self-esteem and people's ability to meet their goals, which leads to unhappiness or even depression. In such cases, receiving the best possible treatment for both the physical problem and the resulting psychological consequences is key to optimal recovery to good mental health.

Abuse

The mental health of abused children is at great risk. Abused children are more likely to experience mental disorders or mental illness during childhood and into adulthood. Abuse may be physical, sexual, psychological or verbal. It may not always be evident or easily recognized. Regardless of the form it takes, abuse cannot be tolerated. Children need to be protected from abuse and helped to overcome its negative effects. Abuse can cause feelings of low self-esteem, lack of self-confidence, depression, isolation and anger—all feelings that impair a child's chance to lead a happy life.

Coping with past or current traumatic experiences such as abuse, bereavement or divorce will strongly influence an individual's mental and emotional state which can in turn have an influence on mental health.

2.2.2.cEnvironmental Factors

An identifiable element in the physical, cultural, demographic, economic, political, regulatory or technological environment that affects the survival operations of an individual is known as environmental factors (Hekin and Polvika, 2015). Environmental factors include the society, peer group, family that affect the mental health of an individual. Social deprivation and poverty can lead to problems such as depression- but they operate through the disillusionment, hopelessness and learned helplessness that constitute a realization that one's action have no effect or purpose. Being abused or traumatized obviously leads to problems, but this association is, again, mediated by the disruption of psychological processes – the ways in which relationships and social intercourse should be governed (British Psychological Society, 2009). Demographics such as age, gender, and ethnicity are important determinants, influencing exposure to risk and protective factors across the life course.

Structural level factors

Include social, economic and cultural factors that are supportive of positive mental health such as safe environment, employment and education.

Community level factors

Include a positive sense of belonging, activities to highlight the embrace diversity, social support and participation in society.

Individual level factors

Such as the ability to manage thoughts and cope with stressors. This may also include substance abuse.

Among environmental factors Larzelere (2000) has also found various parenting practices to be associated with mental health problems such as punitive discipline (yelling, nagging, threatening), inconsistent discipline, lack of warmth or positive involvement, physical aggression (hitting, beating), insufficient monitoring and ineffective problem solving modeling. Parental support plays an important role in parent-child relationship.

2.3 PSYCHOSOCIAL ADJUSTMENT

The term adjustment is often used as a synonym for accommodation and adaptation. The term denotes the results of equilibrium, which may be affected by either of these processes (Monroe, 2007). It is used to emphasize the individual's struggle to get along or survive in his or her social and physical environment.

The concept of adjustment is as old as human race on earth. It is a household word as we often speak of people as being well-adjusted or poorly adjusted. A well-adjusted person is regarded as successful in the art of living. The process of adjustment starts right from birth of the child and continues till his death. Systematic emergence of the concept of Adjustment started with Darwin's (1859) theory of evolution. In biology the term usually employed was adaptation. Darwin maintained that only those organisms most fitted to adapt to the hazards of the physical world survive. Perhaps the most elementary notion as to what constitutes adjusted behaviour is the criteria of survival. Survival as a concept of adjustment suggests that all behaviours may be considered adjustive if and only if they contribute to keeping the individual alive, healthy, and capable of reproducing other members of his species. Biologists have continued to be concerned with the problem of physical adaptation, and many human illnesses are thought to be based on the process of adaptation to the stress of life (Selye, 1956).

Adjustment is a process of directing one's efforts towards modification of behavior and attitudes. Human beings are born with a number of internal needs, e.g. need for food, water, and oxygen etc. Most of these needs are the physiological needs. In the course of development some additional needs emerge. In fact, life is a continuous process of adjusting, self-understanding, personality integration, self-actualization, functional autonomy of motives and frustration.Tolerance contributes to the effective adjustment. Psychologists have interpreted adjustment from two important points of view adjustment as an achievement and adjustment as a process. The first point of view emphasizes the quality or efficiency of adjustment and second lays, emphasis on the process by which an individual adjusts in his external environment. In final analysis the dynamics of adjustment involve a realistic self-appraisal and a whole hearted acceptance of the self. When this is achieved, one is indeed well adjusted.

During recent years, the concept of adjustment as social conformity centres upon the extent to which an individual accepts and abides by group norms, ideals and assumes that the goals of society and the goals of the individual are the same.

Social conformity as a concept may be construed as either a goal or process. The individual who holds this conception is dependent upon the culture in which he/she finds himself and for his/her ideas as to be "adjusted" and "maladjusted" behaviours. The social conformity notion is essentially a continuous conception. In social conformity criterion of adjustment emphasis is placed upon the social behaviour of individuals and the unit of analysis is that of the group of varying sizes with regard to the determination of adjustment, the source of determination is external to the individual. Using the social conformity criterion, one may measure the observable behaviour of individuals with regard to the extent to which it corresponds to the expectations of a particular society (Sechrest and Wallace, 1967). When the individual is a child, the parents make demands upon the growing up child to acquire the proper values and behaviour patterns. When the person is an adult, they continue to have expectations of their marriage, their career, or where and how they live. Wives have certain expectations about their husbands, husbands about their wives, employers about their employees, and children about their parents. These expectations functions as powerful catalyst for the individual (Lazarus, 1961).

The psychologists are more concerned with what might be called "Psychological survival" than physical survival. As in the case of the biological concept of adaptation, human behaviour is interpreted as adjustments to demands or pressures. These demands are primarily social or interpersonal, and they influence the psychological structure and functioning of the person.

Psychologists view the human being as a complex energy system consisting of many subsystems coordinated to maintain the optimum functioning of the organism. As a person participates in his environment, certain changes in the operations of the subsystems are required due to change in the environment or changes originating within certain subsystems. Such a mobilization of energy tends to· persist until either the conditions which aroused it have been neutralised or removed, or a reorganization and harmony of the subsystems can be effected that will restore efficient general functioning to the organism. Changes in behaviour in response to these demands upon the organism are termed adjustment (**Sreenivasan &Weinberger,** 2016).

2.3.1Theories of Psychosocial Adjustment

2.3.1.aPsychoanalytical Theory

One of the modern pioneers in the study of human adjustment and probably the most influential of any time was Sigmund Freud (1856-1939). From his work with emotionally disturbed people Freud (1895) developed his psychoanalytical theory, in which the basic "driving forces" are biologically based, undifferentiated sexual and aggressive energies or drives. These drives, which are the core of traditional psychoanalytical theory, are the "bad motives". In the process of socialization one learns socially acceptable ways to discharge these biological energies. In addition, he suggest that a portion of energy comes to be controlled by the ego, which is responsible for one's rational and mature development of personality.

Neo Freudians (Karen Horney 1950; Carl Jung 1953; Erik Erikson 1960; Alfred Adler 1964) placed less emphasis on the biological or innate components of basic human needs, and put their focus more on needs produced by the demands of the interpersonal and social environment. The individual makes an effort to adjust to all these demands.

2.3.1.bHumanistic and Existentialism Theory

The Humanistic theorists like Carl Rogers (1959) and Maslow (1967, 1970) suggested that people are not innately evil, but are innately good. Like Freud, Maslow also suggested that human nature is determined biologically, but they came to the opposite conclusion, that all people have the potential for positive growth, if favorable environment is provided to them and they ultimately reach the state of self-actualization. According to him the best and most well-adjusted people are those who have developed successfully through the basic stages and reached the highest stage of self-actualization in which their basic potential's are completely expressed.

A specific phenomenological position regarding adjustment is offered by existential psychology. Existentialists (Carl Rogers1902-1987; Combs and Snygg, 1949) argue that we are each individually and uniquely responsible for our own destiny. Each person, thus, actively decides or is continually deciding, upon a particular path of action. For the existentialists, life is a constant series of decision some of which may appear trivial or inconsequential. It is the pattern of these decisions, and their consequences that really determine the quality of the individual's adjustment. In making these decisions the individual's "Free Will" is emphasized above environmental influence, past experience or internal psychological or biological states. Thus, each person is seen as actively deciding his or her own fate and, therefore, responsible for the consequences of the decision that are made.

2.3.1.cBehavioral Theory of Adjustment

Behaviorism is an approach of psychology that combines the elements of philosophy, methodology and theory. It emerged in early 20th century and was proposed by Thorndike (1905) Watson (1913) and Skinner (1937). According to this model adjustment is the efficiency of the individual which helps to generate positive consequences and avoids the negative consequences. Behavior is universal that assumes that an individual is basically responding to environmental stimuli (Adam 1975). Behavior psychology developed in part as a reaction against psychodynamic theory. It is a theory of learning based on the idea that all behaviours are acquired through conditioning. Conditioning occurs through interaction with the environment. Behaviourists believe that our responses to environmental stimuli shape our actions. Well-adjusted people are they who have learnt behaviors that help them to deal successfully with life's challenges.

2.3.2 Aspects of Adjustment

There are many and untouchable fields in the sphere of life, but some hold prime position in an individual's life sphere such as home, health, social, emotional and educational fields. The way of adjustment of an individual in these fields influences him to create his personality according to his type of adjustment. Some important areas of adjustment are as follows:

2.3.2.a Home Adjustment

The degree of adjustment of an individual at home exhibits in his behavior with others. If one is well adjusted at home, most probably he must be well adjusted socially because the adjustments in different fields of life are related and effective to each other. A well-adjusted child will be more cherished and happy in comparison to the poor-adjusted

2.3.2.b Health Adjustment

Health also plays a prime role in the development of one's personality. Sound health is the source of satisfaction and adjustment. The person should be physically as well as mentally healthy. Physically and mentally healthy person always feels well-adjusted in society then the unhealthy one. An unhealthy person is usually a maladjusted person. Physically and mentally healthy person feels secure and contented in his or her life.

2.3.2.c Social Adjustment

Areas of social adjustment are influenced by social maturity of the person. Maturity in social relationship means to establish good relations with family, neighbors, playmates, fellows and other members of the society. Socially, mature person behaves in accordance with social norms, customs and traditions. Socially adjusted personnever engages in anti-social activities.

2.3.2.d Emotional Adjustment

A balanced personality is one which is emotionally adjusted. Every instinct is followed by some emotion and in this way various emotions play an important role in the personality of an individual. An emotionally stable person may be well adjusted and emotionally unstable conditions causes mental disorders and maladjustment. Emotional adjustment is essential for creating a sound personality. Physical, intellectual, mental and esthetical adjustments are possible when emotional adjustment is made. Emotional adjustment is followed by the social adjustment. Such person's activities are socially beneficial and individually helpful in maintaining effective personality.

2.3.2.e Educational Adjustment

The term educational adjustment refers to education, as helping, growth and change in an individual so that they may be better equipped to deal with the various factors of the environment affecting him. Educational adjustment provides an individual to rise up, to improve his personality, to change his behavior and to make him able to cope with every situation of life. Educational adjustment is followed by vocational adjustment; both of these are correlated to each other.

2.3.2.fSchool Adjustment

School adjustment is the process of adapting to the role of being a student and to various aspects of the school environment. School adjustment has been construed historically in terms of children's academic progress or achievement (Birch & Ladd, 1996). This outcome is important, but being very limited it narrows the search for precursors and events in children's environments that may affect adjustment. On a broader level, we might think of adjustment as involving not only children's progress and achievement but also their attitudes toward school, anxieties, loneliness, social support, and academic motivation (e.g., engagement, avoidance, absences) (Birch & Ladd, 1996; Roeser, 1998; Roeser et al., 1998).

2.3.3Factors Affecting Adjustment

The factors which affect adjustment are listed below:

2.3.3.aHeredity Factors

Heredityis the biological process responsible for passing on physical traits from one generation to another. It includes things such as genetics, parenting, experiences, friends, family, education, and relationships. It can also refer to inheriting characteristics from your parents, or it can refer more broadly to the passing on of genetic factors from one generation to the next. It is received by every individual at the time of conception. Every individual on this earth is different from the other. Sometimes there may be problem due to heredity factor. The two most basic influences on social behavior are genes (the chemical instructions that people inherit from their parents' DNA) and the environment (all other, non-inherited factors). Individual differences in emotion regulation in toddlerhood are influenced by genetic and non-shared environmental factors, and importantly, that common geneticeffects contribute to the association between emotion regulation and working memory (Wang, 2013).

2.3.3.b Physiological Factors

Physiological factors are things related to one's physical body that affect his/her thinking. For example, when your body's chemistry is off, due to unbalanced nutrition, dehydration, alcohol, etc., the neurotransmitters that control your thinking processes can be affected. Physiological factors also include changes to the brain's structure due to injuries, extended periods of inactivity, or physical stress. There are some common needs of every individual. These include hunger, thrust, shelter, clothes etc. Maslow (1976) has categorized individual needs into five categories. These five categories are physiological needs, safety needs, social needs or needs for belongingness, esteem needs and self actualization needs. If basic physiological and safety needs are not fulfilled, the individual feels frustrated and this is one of the causes of maladjustment.

2.3.3.cEnvironmental Factors

Environmentis everything that is around us. It can be living or non-living things. It includes physical, chemical and other natural forces. Living things live in their environment. They constantly interact with it and adapt themselves to conditions in their environment. The external factors of an individual such as family, school and society also affect adjustment. Any adverse conditions in these factors become the cause of maladjustment. So the children who do not get love, respect, security and acceptance from the primary caregivers in childhood are the most maladjusted as adults.

2.4ACADEMICPERFORMANCE

Academic Performance or achievement is the educational goal that is achieved by a student. It is defined as excellence in all academic disciplines, in class as well as co- curricular activities. It includes excellence in sporting behavior, confidence, communication skills, punctuality, arts, culture and the like which can be achieved only when an individual is well adjusted.

According to Cambridge University Reporter (2003) academic performance is frequently defined in terms of examination performance. Academic achievement refers to what the student has learned or what skills the student has acquired and is usually measured through assessments like standardized tests, performance assessment and portfolio assessment.

Pandey (2008) defined academic achievement as the performance of the student's in the subjects they study in the school. It is directly related to students growth and development of knowledge in educational situation where teaching, learning takes place.

Sharma, Manika and Khatoon (2011) defined academic achievement as the outcome of the training imparted to students by the teacher in school situation.

Hence, academic performance is the maximum performance in all the activities at school after a period of training. It reflects the complete child as it is not related to a single instance, but to human growth, cognitive, emotional, social and physical development. Therefore, academic achievement should be considered to be a multifaceted construct that comprises different domains of learning which influences one's vocational career after education. Besides the relevance for an individual, academic achievement is of utmost importance for the wealth of a nation and its prosperity. There is a strong association between a society's level of academic achievement and positive socio-economic development.

2.4.1 Models of Academic Performance

Different models have been put forward by theorist to represent the complex interrelationships that exist among the predictors of academic achievement. Noticeable among them are the following.

2.4.1.a The Carroll Model

In 1963, John Carroll proposed a model for school learning. Learning was defined as function of efforts spent in relation to efforts needed. In this model, the achievement of a student or the degree of learning effectiveness is defined as a function of the actual time needed for learning and the time actually spent for learning. The effect of both variables on the degree of learning effectiveness has been expressed in a functional equation. This model is time based.

According to Reeves (1997) Carroll's model includes six elements:

Academic Achievement is the output (as measured by various sorts' standard achievement tests).

Aptitude is the main explanatory variable defined as the "the amount of time a student needs to learn a given task, unit of instruction, or curriculum to an acceptable criterion of mastery under optimal conditions of instruction and student motivation" (Carroll, 1989). "High aptitude is indicated when a student needs a relatively small amount of time to learn, low aptitude is indicated when a student needs much more than average time to learn (Carrol: 1989).

Opportunity to learn: Amount of time available for learning both in class and within homework. Carroll (1998) notes that "frequently, opportunity to learn is less than required in view of the student's aptitude".

Ability to understand instruction: relates to learning skills, information needed to understand, and language comprehension.

Quality of instruction: refers to the effectiveness with which the unit of instruction is actually delivered.

Perseverance: Amount of time a student is willing to spend on a given task or unit of instruction. This is an operational and measurable definition for motivation for learning.

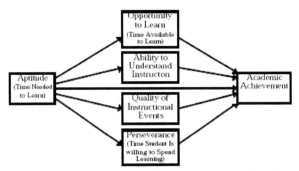

Figure 2.1:Carroll's (1963, 1989) Model of School Learning

2.4.1.bBruner's Cognitive Developmental Theory of Instruction

Bruner (1966) has specified four features in his normative theory of instruction, these are:

Predisposition to learn - A theory of instruction must be concerned with the experiences and context that will tend to make the child willing and able to learn when he enters the school.

Structure of knowledge - A theory of instruction should specify the ways in which body of knowledge should be structured so that it can be most readily grasped by the learner.

Sequence of instruction – A theory of instruction should specify the most effective sequences to present the material.

Reinforcement – A theory of instruction should specify the nature and pacing of rewards, moving from extrinsic rewards to intrinsic one.

2.4.1.cThe Cooley-LeinhardtModel

This model by Cooley-Leinhardt (1975) focuses on the relationship between school practices and school performance. The criteria variable being predicted includes both academic achievement and attitudes towards school, peers and teachers. School Performance is a function of the following constructs: initial abilities, opportunity, motivators, structure and instructional events.

2.4.1.d The Harnischfeger-Wiley Model

Harnischfeger & Wiley (1976) model is both school achievement and student achievement. Theory proposed the model which encompasses background characteristics of teacher and pupil and also curriculum plus institutional factors, teaching-learning processes (includes teacher activities and pupil pursuits) and outcomes. Central to the mode; is the explicit recognition that all pupil outcomes are directly meditated through pupil pursuits. Thus, teacher's behavior can influence learning only as they affect those pursuits.

2.4.1.e The Bloom Model

This model given by Bloom (1976) describes two types of prerequisites to learning: the learner's cognitive entry behaviors (which includes reading comprehension, learning objectives and verbal intelligence) and affective entry characteristics (attitude towards subject matter, toward school and self concept as a learner). Quality of instruction is reflected in the cues (clarity of presentation and explanation), reinforcements (praise and blame, encouragement and other rewards), feedback and correctives (sequences of tasks and learning units), and is also indicated by participation or the degree of overt and covert involvement of students in the learning task.

2.4.1.f The Gagne Model

Gagne (1977) described eight types of learning, their products and the conditions necessary to produce them. The five major categories of learning are verbal information, intellectual skills, cognitive strategies, attitude and motor skills. These five represent what is learned. Each of these categories of outcome requires different types of conditions for learning and retention to occur.

Gagne (1977) further posits eight internal phases through which all learning proceeds and are derived from information –processing model. This is (1) activating motivation, (2) informing learner of the objective, (3) directing attention, (4) stimulating recall, (5) providing learning guidance, (6) enhancing retention, (7) promoting transfer of learning, (8) eliciting performance and providing feedback.

2.4.1.g Model of Academic Competence (MAC)

DiPerna and Elliott (2002, 2005) in their Model of Academic Competence (MAC) defined academic competence as "a multidimensional construct consisting of the skills, attitudes, and behaviours of learners that contribute to success in the classrooms". Academic competence includes the domains of academic skills and academic enablers. "Academic skills are the basic and complex skills that are the primary focus of academic instruction in elementary and secondary schools.In contrast, academic enablers are attitudes and behaviours that allow a learner to participate in, and ultimately benefit from, academic instruction in the classroom" Both the MAC academic skill and enabler domains include narrower and specific skills and behaviour. The academic domain reflects the acquired declarative and procedural knowledge domains of language-based achievement (reading and writing), mathematics, and critical thinking.DiPerna and Elliott's (2000) research led to the identification of four specific categories of academic enabling behaviors—interpersonal skills, motivation, study skills, and engagement.

2.4.1.hSelf-Regulated learning Model

Self-regulated learning (SRL) Model includes the cognitive, Meta cognitive, behavioral, motivational, and emotional/affective aspects of learning. It is, therefore, an extraordinary umbrella under which a considerable number of variables that influence learning (e.g., self-efficacy, volition, and cognitive strategies) are studied within a comprehensive and holistic approach. For that reason, SRL has become one of the most important areas of research within educational psychology.

According to the review of six self-regulated learning models by Panadero (2017) most models are compounded of three phases: preparatory, performance and appraisal. As stated by Panadero (2017) "(a) preparatory, which includes task analysis, planning, activation of goals, and setting goals; (b) performance, in which the actual task is done while monitoring and controlling the progress of performance; and (c) appraisal, in which the student reflects, regulates, and adapts for future performances.

2.4.2Theories of Academic Performance

Apart from the models discussed above, different researchers have tried to explain the concept of academic performance by giving different theories:

2.4.2.aWalberg's Theory of Educational Productivity

Walberg's (1981) theory of educational productivity, which is one of the few empirically testedtheories of school learning based on an extensive review and integration of over 3,000 studies (DiPerna, Volpe & Stephen, 2002).According to the theory if one wants to increase educational productivity and efficiency, educational process goals as well as achievement goals must be considered. Educational process goals are interpreted to include student perceptions of the social environment, creativity, self-concept, participation in extra-curricular activities, and interest in subject matter. Ignoring these perceptions and experiences in favor of traditional goals measured by test scores will decrease motivation and ultimately lower educational achievement. Many Educational experiments and psychological theories of education fail to produce desired educational outcomes because they do not clearly identify, define, and measure educational variables.

2.4.2.bThe Triarchic Theory of Intellectual Abilities

According to the theory of intellectual abilities given by Sternberg (1985) three kinds of intellectual abilities exists, namely, analytical, creative and practical abilities. He states that the more we teach and assess students based on a broader set of abilities, the more racially, ethically and socioeconomically diverse our achievers will be. Further, Sternberg emphasizes that student's learning and thinking styles together with their ability levels play an important role in student performance.

2.4.3Factors Affecting Academic Performance

Academic achievement can be influenced by a variety of factors from simple demographic factors such as age, gender and family socio economic status to more variable factors like the quality of the teaching faculty at a student's school and the way that students with special needs are grouped together. Different educational theorists in order to explain factors that affect academic achievement has given different viewpoints which are given below:

Laurel, Wong, chan, and Safiyyah, (2008) have appropriately divided the factors influencing student performance into two categories1) academic factors and (2) non-academic factors. Academic factors include teaching methods, self-learning efforts, and student's previous results, whilst, non-academic performance are those like health factors, personal factors, financial factors, and even the environment and its compositionlikepeople and culture (Laurelet.al., 2008).

Ghazvini and Khajehpour (2011) stated that it is important to know about the factors that affect academic performance so that it could be used to influence the academic motivation and ultimately increase the academic success of the students. They have focused on the following three factors that affect academic achievement:

Locus of Control

It is conceptualized on a dynamic bipolar continuum spanning from internal to external. Internal locus of control is characterized by the belief that consequences are a result of one's own behaviour. In order words, individuals who believe that their successes or failure result from their own behaviours possess an internal locus of control.Whereas external locus off control is characterized by the belief that consequences are a result of fate, luck or powerful others. Thus, individuals with an external locus of control might not take responsibility for their own actions and behaviours. Moreover, they tend to be reactive and aiod distressing situations.

Self-Concept

Byrne (1984) concluded that self-concept is a multi-dimensional construct, having one general facet and specific facets, one of which is, academic self-concept. Self-concept is the set of perceptions or reference points that the subject has about himself.It is the set of characteristics, attributes, qualities and deficiencies, capacities and limits, values and relationships that the subjects knows to be descriptive of himself and which he perceives as data concerninghis identity (Hamachek, 1981). It is the set of knowledge and attitudes that we have about ourselves; the perceptions that the individual assigns to himself and characteristics or attributes that we use to describe our-selves. The importance of self-concept stems from its notable contribution to personality formation. Academic self-concept reflects descriptive as well as evaluative aspects. Moreover, self-perceptions associated with academic self-concept tend to focus on scholastic competence, rather than attitudes. A student's self-perception of academic ability or achievement will affecttheir school performance.

Learning Strategies

Weinstein, Husman and Deirking (2000) describe learning strategies as tools used in the service of goals. They further define learning strategies as any thoughts, behaviours, beliefs or emotions that facilitate the acquisition, understanding, or later transfer of new knowledge and skills. Tessmer and Jonassen (1988) have divided learning strategies into two categories, i.e., primary and support strategies. Primary strategies work with information to be learned and have to do with our cognition. Support strategies are all aimed at improving general cognitive functioning and have to do with our self-regulation for learning.

Pintrinch and De Groot (1990) have best encompassed the complexity of motivational processes at the academic level where they have distinguished three general categories of relevant constructs for motivation in educational contexts: an expectation component, which includes student's beliefs about their ability to complete a task; a value component, including students' goals and beliefs about the task's importance and interest; and an affective component, including affective-emotional consequences derived from completing a task as well as results of success or failure.

Further, gender has also been recognized as one of the factor that determines the difference in self-regulated learning. Lightbody, Siann, Stocks and Walsh (1996) and Georgiou (1999) stated that girls tend to give more emphasis to effort when explaining their performance and boys appeal more to ability and luck as causes of their academic achievement.

North et.al., (2012) have indentified three major factors that affect the academic achievement:

Self-Efficacy and Cognitive Ability

This concept is based on the assumption that negative attitude toward learning are attributed to lack of basic skills in learning, weak mastery of language skills and poor self-efficacy that influence the success or failure of the students. Self-efficacy is the belief that one possesses the capabilities to organize, plan and carry out the courses of action required to manage situation at hand. Cognitive ability includes grasping the basic learning capabilities which are literacy and numeracy. Examination of these basic skills is imperative as the incompetence of such skills could be a hindrance for subject matter mastery.

Parental Participation and Family Support

The student's family institution marks the beginning of a student's learning habits, pattern and culture. Lumsden (1994) stated that children's home environment shapes the initial constellation of attitudes they develop toward learning. When parents nurture their children's natural curiosity about the world by welcoming their questions, encouraging exploration and familiarizing with resources that can enlarge their world, they are giving the children the message that learning is worthwhile and frequently fun and satisfying. Home environment and early experience help to create curiosity, help build self-efficacy and shape the individual's behaviour. Sumari, Hussain and Siraj(2010) stated that factors like parent's expectations, home environment, discipline and parent involvement also affect student's achievement. A well functional family could create a positive climate in the family institution in which the dynamic communication and effective relationship could determine the educational climate in the family, and in turn influence the academic results.

The Role of Teachers and School

Teachers and school play pertinent role in the capabilities development and acade4mic achievement of the student. Teachers are seen as the main source of learning in schools especially in ensuring the student's success. Learning process could be enjoyable where the learning approach used could attract the student's attention, develop interest in learning and ensure full participation in the classroom. Thus, pedagogical approaches need to be well structured and systematic for effective learning to take place.

Tanfaraju, Ho. Chee, Koon, Yi and Mann (2013) have given six factors for academic achievement:

Academic Performance

Academic performance is measured in terms of past examination performance, performance in midterms and failure in modules (Tan and Yates, 2007). Academic success is important because it is strongly linked to positive outcomes.

Teaching Method

It is the role played by the teachers in the teaching process and technology used in the process (Jefferson and Kent, 2001).

Time Management

It has been defined as a behavioural skill that is important in organizing study load (Talib and Sansgiry, 2012) which includes advance planning, work prioritizing and test preparation. Effective time management strategies have been found to increase academic (Campbell and Svenson 1992; Powell, 2004).

Attendance of Students

Attendance refers to the actual school performance of pupil during the school days (Jones, 2006) and a measure of class involvement (Howard, 2005). Nasari and Ahmed (2006) found that high absenteeism will lead to degradation of academic performance.

Sleep

It is defined as an academic, repetitive and reversible behaviour that serves several different functions as repair and learning consolidation and restorative processes (Curcio, Ferrar and Gennaro, 2006). They found that sleep loss and sleep fragmentation could negatively affect the learning and memory and reduce academic achievement. It further reflected that poor sleep quality could seriously impair the student's behavioral performace and cognitive functioning.

Racial Ideology

Research by Sanders (1997) and Smalls, White, Chavius and Selller (2007) have found that racial discrimination leads to lower academic performance.

Thus, from the above mentioned models, theories and factors, it can be concluded that the most important component for academic achievement is cognitive and learning abilities of the student themselves. But, as mentioned by Walberg (1981)and Khajehpour and Ghazvini (2011) parental involvement also plays an important rold in academic achievement of the students.

2.5 PARENT-CHILD RELATIONSHIP

Relationships between parents and children are among the many close relationships that individuals experience throughout their life. Parent–child relationships are important because they are central to the lives of both parents and children, and provide one of the most important environments in which children develop as individuals and as functioning members of their culture (Hartup & Laursen, 1991).

Parent–child relationships are complex and multidimensional. They vary over time, differ from the perspective of the parent and of the child, and differ from one situation to another, and so on. Depending on one's theoretical perspective, there are many ways to describe the central features or dimensions of parent–child relationships. For example, discussions of family relationships (e.g., Noller & Fitzpatrick, 1993) typically cover areas such as affection, conflict, power and control. When other close relationships are discussed (e.g., Canary & Emmers-Sommer, 1997), intimacy and control have been given special treatment. Duck (1992) emphasized communication, including verbal and non-verbal communication, as central elements in a relationship.

The Oxford English Dictionary (1996) defined parenting as the single - minded unconditional desire to provide a loving, caring Home.

Hodges, Finnegan, and Perry (1999) raised connectedness/closeness and independence (autonomy) as major issues in parent–child relationships.

Maccoby (1999) discussed important questions about the conceptualization of parent–child relationships in terms of intra-individual differences. The notion here is that within the overall parent–child relationship there are likely to be differences according to the context or domain of the interactions. For example, if the domain pertains to discipline, one set of "rules" or relationship qualities will be apparent. On the other hand, if the context is one of play and games, then another set of relationship characteristics will be appropriate. Contexts differ and the roles of parent and child are multiple. Thus, there are multiple parent–child relationships rather than a single parent–child relationship domain.

Crockett, Brown, Russell and Shen (2007) derived the meaning of parent-child relationship in adolescent as having "open communication, instrumental and emotional support, indirect expressions of care, parental control, and valued relationship qualities".

The parent-child relationship refers to the bond that the parents form with their children. Of the many different relationships people form over the course of the life span, the relationship between parent and child is among the most important. The quality of the parent-child relationship is affected by the parent's age, experience, and self-confidence, the stability of the parents' marriage, and the unique characteristics of the child compared with those of the parent. The parent-child relationship consists of a combination of behaviors, feelings, and expectations that are unique to a particular parent and a particular child. The relationship involves the full extent of a child's development. Parent-child relationship is a combination of behaviors, feelings, and expectations that are unique to a particular parent and a particular child and the relationship that evolves contributes significantly to the overall development of the child (Linwood, 2006).

2.5.1 Theoriesof Parent-Child Relationship

Several theories have been proposed to explain the psychological significance of parent-child relationship and why they are strongly linked with children's well-being (Sears 1957; Maccoby; and Mortin; 1983; Maccoby, 1992).

In the first half of twentieth century, research on these broad theoretical positions was patchy, but did not inhibit strong views being advanced about the ways that parents should approach the task of parenting. Much contemporary research in parent-child relationship can be traced to the following dominant prospectives:

2.5.1.aSymbolic Interaction Theory

Symbolic Interaction theory was given by Cooley (1902) and Mead (1934).It is a school of thought in sociology that explains social behaviour in terms of how people interact with each other via symbols; in this view, social structures are best understood in terms of such individual interactions. The central theme of symbolic interaction theory is that human life is lived in the symbolic domain. Symbols are culturally derived social objects having shared meanings that are created and maintained in social interaction. Through language and communication, symbols provide the means by which reality is constructed. Reality is primarily a social product, and all that is humanly consequential—self, mind, society, culture—emerges from and is dependent on symbolic interactions for its existence. Even the physical environment is relevant to human conduct *mainly* as it is interpreted through symbolic systems.

2.5.1.b Psychoanalytic Theory

Freud (1938) elaborated his argument around unresolved conflict between mother and child, fears of an experience of physical and psychological abandonment and the consequence of these for abnormal mental health. In psychosexual theory of development, for instance, Freud placed special emphasis on parental relationships and later psychopathology. Psychoanalysts believed that early mother-child relationships form the prototype of all future relationships and the outcome of adolescents' development depends on their ego-strength.

2.5.1.cObject-relation Theory

Object relations theory in psychoanalytic psychology is the process of developing a psyche in relation to others in the environment during childhood. Ronald Fairbairn (1952) independently formulated the theory of object relations. Based on psychodynamic theory, the object relations theory suggests that the way people relate to others and situations in their adult lives are shaped by family experiences during infancy. For example, an adult who experienced neglect or abuse in infancy would expect similar behaviour from others who remind them of the neglectful or abusive parent from their past. These images of people and events turn into objects in the unconscious that the "self" carries into adulthood, and they are used by the unconscious to predict people's behaviour in their social relationships and interactions. The first "object" in someone is usually an internalized image of one's mother. Internal objects are formed by the patterns in one's experience of being taken care of as a baby, which may or may not be accurate representations of the actual, external caretakers. Objects are usually internalized images of one's mother, father, or primary caregiver.

2.5.1.dAttachment theory

Attachment theory in psychology originates with the seminal work of John Bowlby (1958).In the 1930's Bowlby worked as a psychiatrist in a Child Guidance Clinic in London, where he treated many emotionally disturbed children.This experience led Bowlby to consider the importance of the child's relationship with their mother in terms of their social, emotional and cognitive development.A history of consistent and sensitive care with the parent is therefore expected to lead to the child developing a model of self and others as loveable and loving/helpful (Cicchetti et al., 2000; Bakermans-Kranenburg et al., 2003). Attachment is a deep and enduring emotional bond that connects one person to another across time and space (Ainsworth, 1973; Bowlby, 1969). Attachment does not have to be reciprocal.One person may have an attachment with an individual which is not shared.Attachment is characterized by specific behaviors in children, such as seeking proximity with the attachment figure when upset or threatened (Bowlby, 1969). Attachment behavior in adults towards the child includes responding sensitively and appropriately to the child's needs.Such behavior appears universal across cultures. Attachment theory provides an explanation of how the parent-child relationship emerges and influences subsequent development of the child over a life span.

2.5.1.eSocial Learning Theory

This is one of the most influential theories of parent–child relationships, and closely associated with the ideas and findings of Bandura (e.g. Bandura, 1977). Social Learning Theory argues that child's real-life experiences and an exposure directly or indirectly shapes his/her behavior. For Patterson (1969, 1996) and many others there is a focus on traditional behavioral principles of reinforcement and conditioning. The fundamental tenet is that moment-to-moment exchanges are crucial; if a child receives an immediate reward for his/her behavior, such as getting parental attention or approval, then he/she is likely to repeat that behavior again. Other advocates have expanded this focus to consider the cognitive or 'mindful' processes that underlie the parent's behavior (Bugenthal et al., 1989; Dix, 1992) and its effects on children (Dodge et al., 1995). Whether the assessment and conceptual focus is on behavior or cognitions, the model suggests that children learn strategies about managing their emotions, resolving disputes and engaging with others not only from their experiences, but also from the way their own reactions were responded to. For younger children especially, the primary source of these experiences is in the context of the parent–child relationship and the family environment.

2.5.1.fParental Acceptance –Rejection Theory (PAR Theory)

PAR Theory, proposed by Rohner (1975, 1986) is an evidence based theory of socialization which suggests that children all over the world need to be loved by parents and other significant caregivers. Probably this need is biologically based.

PAR Theory predicts that parental rejection has consistent negative effects on the psychological adjustment and on behavioral functioning of both children and adults worldwide. This has been confirmed by a vast research literature (Rohner 1975; Rohner 1980; Khaleque and Rohner; 2002). According to Rohner, Khaleque and Cournoyer (2011) the more (acceptance, warmth, affection, care, comfort, concern, nurturance, support or simply love) children receive from their parents or caregivers the more positive influence will be on children's development and the more rejection (absence or significant withdrawal of warmth, affection, care and presence of physically and psychologically hurtful behavior and affects), the more negative influence it will have on children's development.

Parents can express their love or lack of love in three principal ways. They can be i) cold and unaffectionate, ii) hostile and aggressive or iii) indifferent and neglecting. Additionally, parental rejection can be subjectively experienced by individualism in the form of undifferentiated rejection. Undifferentiated rejection refers to the feeling that one's parents are cold and affectionate, hostile and aggressive or indifferent and neglecting.

2.5.1.gMindful Parenting Model

Mindful Parenting Model has been described as a fundamental parenting skill or practice (Kabat-Zinn and Kabat Zinn, 1997 and Steinberg 2004), and it has been proposed that fostering everyday mindfulness in the context of parenting and parent training is one avenue for improving the effectiveness of parenting interventions (Dumas 2005). However, empirical evidence on the role of mindfulness in parenting is sparse and a comprehensive model of mindful parenting has not yet been developed. The model of mindful parentingoffer extends the concepts and practices of *mindfulness,* defined here as "the awareness that emerges through paying attention, on purpose, in the present moment, and non-judgmentally to the unfolding of experience moment by moment" (Kabat-Zinn 2003), to the social context of parent–child relationships.

2.5.2ParentingStyles

Parenting style has a big impact on how children develop into adults, and there are important implications for their future success. Parents influence their child's social skills directly, indirectly and through management of their child's activities. A parenting style is a psychological construct representing standard strategies that parents use in their child rearing. The quality of parenting can be more essential than the quantity of time spent with the child. Parenting styles are the representation of how parents respond and demand to their children. There are various theories and opinions on the best ways to rear children, as well as differing levels of time and effort that parents are willing to invest.

Types of Parenting Styles

There are four major recognized parenting styles: authoritative, neglectful, permissive, and authoritarian. Each one carries different characteristics and brings about different reactions in the children which they are used to (Mgbemere and Telles 2013).

Authoritarian Parenting

Authoritarian parenting is widely regarded as the most effective and beneficial parenting style for normal children. Authoritarian parents are marked by the high expectations that they have of their children, but temper these expectations with a support for their children as well. This type of parenting creates the healthiest environment for a growing child, and helps to foster a productive relationship between parent and child.

Neglectful Parenting

Neglectful parenting is one of the most harmful styles of parenting that can be used on a child. Neglectful parents and the children involved in the situation need assistance so that they can get back on track to having a healthy and communicative relationship within the family. Neglectful parenting is damaging to children, because they have no trust foundation with their parents from which to explore the world. Beyond that, children who have a negative or absent relationship with their parent will have a harder time forming relationships with other people, particularly children of their age.

Democratic Parenting

There is a third style known as "democratic parenting." Rather than the parent running the show (authoritarian) or the child steering the family (permissive), democratic household are based on respect for both the parent and the child. This style represents a consistent path forward, rather than inconsistent swinging from side to side.

Permissive Parenting

Permissive parenting, also known as indulgent parenting is another potentially harmful style of parenting. These parents are responsive but not demanding. These parents tend to be lenient while trying to avoid confrontation. The benefit of this parenting style is that they are usually very nurturing and loving. The negatives, however, outweigh this benefit. Few rules are set for the children of permissive parents, and the rules are inconsistent when they do exist. This lack of structure causes these children to grow up with little self-discipline and self-control.

Authoritative Parenting

Authoritarian parenting, also called strict parenting, is characterized by parents who are demanding but not responsive. Authoritarian parents allow for little open dialogue between parent and child and expect children to follow a strict set of rules and expectations. They usually rely on punishment to demand obedience or teach a lesson.

2.5.3 Factors Affecting Parent-Child Relationship

There are certain factors which affect the quality of relationship that children share with their parents. Some of the factors can enhance the quality of parent-child relationship and some can have detrimental effect on them.

The major factors affecting parent-child relationship are:

Parental Relationship

Relationship that the mother and father share amongst themselves has been found to predict child's well-being in the domains of social competence, academic performance, psychosocial development, and problem behavior. Parents of academically motivated, achieving children have cordial relationship with each other. Parent's involvement, encouragement and guidance help whereas a harsh attitude, like being dominant or indulgent, hinders the overall development of the child.

Socio-Economic Status

Socio-economic status of a family is reflected by the parental occupational status and the level of income that parents earn. Socio-economic status also plays a significant role in parent-child relationship. Unemployed or low income parents tend to see themselves as incapable because they cannot meet the needs of their children and family. Inadequate resources create conflict in the family. Such a state of affairs may influence the parent-child relationship and subsequently the holistic development of a child.

Type of Family/Family size

It is reasonable to expect parents from nuclear family to be able to devote more time to their children than those from joint /extended family settings, thus, children from larger families may have negative effects on the quality of parent-child relationship.The structural difference between the joint family and nuclear family leads to different interaction patterns among members of the two family types. Children in joint families are often indulged and overprotected, which encourages child's dependence on the mother and other family members. In nuclear families, the child is in more direct contact with his or her parents, and the number of adult role models decreases. As compared to children from joint families, children from nuclear families are encouraged to function in an individualized manner, take initiative and act independently. Father play an important role in nuclear family since they are often more approachable and psychotically available to their children (Bisht and Sinha, 1981).

Joint Family

In joint families the network of relatives acts as a close-knit community. Joint families can include, aside from parents and their children spouses of children, cousins, aunts, uncles and foster children/adopted children etc.In Joint families workload is equally shared among the members. The women are often housewives and cook for the entire family. The patriarch of the family (often the oldest male member) lays down the rules, works (if not retired) and arbitrates disputes. They are also responsible in teaching the younger children their mother tongue, manners and etiquette.

Nuclear family

The term nuclear family developed in the western world to distinguish the family group consisting of parents, most commonly a father and mother, and their children. Nuclear families can be of any size, as long as the family can support itself and there are only parents and children. According to Merriam-Webster, the term dates back to 1947 and is therefore relatively new, although nuclear family structures themselves date back thousands of years. Traditionally, families in India have been classified as joint in nature. Joint families consist of one or more married couples residing with their children and other close relatives, such as grandparents, aunts, and uncles, all in one home. A nuclear family structure, which is becoming increasingly common,constitutes a single married couple and their children (Ahuja, 1993; Bisht & Sinha, 1981; Muttalib, 1990). The structural differences between the joint family and the nuclear family lead to different interaction patterns among members of the two family types. Children in joint families are often indulged and overprotected, which encourages child's dependence on the mother and other family members. In nuclear families, the child is in more direct contact with his or her parents, and the number of adult role models decreases. As compared to children from joint families, children from nuclear families are encouraged to function in an individualized manner, take initiative, and act independently. Fathers play an important role in nuclear families since they are often more approachable and psychologically available to their children (Bisht and Sinha, 1981).

Birth Order

It was Alfred Adler (1870–1937) who first recognized birth order as a significant factor in personality development. Adler believed that "even though children have the same parents and grow up in nearly the same family setting, they do not have identical social environments" (Hjelle & Ziegler 1992). Leman's (2000) research on birth order personality characteristics supports Adler's findings in most respects.

Leman (2000) reports that oldest borns tend to be conscientious, well organized, serious, goal-oriented achieving, believers in authority, reliable, perfectionists and self-reliant. He also states that these seemingly positive, motivated characteristics help the oldest child to succeed academically and professionally, but the same characteristics can damage close relationships they have with others. Leman (2000) disagrees in some respect with Adler when it comes to the characteristics and reputation of only children. According to him the only children tend to be confident, perfectionist, organized, ambitious, logical and scholarly. Though only children can be self-centred, it is not to the extreme that the existing stereotypes indicate. Furthermore, only children take some of these traits, namely perfectionism, into their interpersonal relationships. This result in high expectations for anyone an only child comes in contact with (Leman, 2000).

Middle born children have a list of contradictory personality characteristics: loner/sociable, impatient/laid-back, and aggressive/conflict-avoider. This suggests that middle children do not have a certain list of general characteristics like the other birth orders. Leman (2000) did say that middle born children tend to be mediators and are choosy about who they confide in. These children also are one of the most monogamous birth orders, who are motivated to make their marriages and families work. Middle born children also tend to have fewer problems than first-born/only children. All of these qualities affect their relationships with people (Leman 2000).

Youngest children tend to be charming, people-oriented, tenacious, affectionate and attention-seeking. They also tend to just "do" things – without thinking about the consequences of their actions. This is a trait that would come into play during relationships as well (Leman 2000).

CHAPTER-3
REVIEW OF LITERATURE

Review of related literature is an essential aspect of research. It involves synthetic and synoptic understanding of the research works already conducted in the same field over a period of time. It provides some insight regarding strong points and limitations of the previous studies and enables the researcher to improve his own investigation (Panigrahi, 1999).

This chapter is organized as follows: First section covers review of studies pertaining to Internet communication, more specifically adolescent and Internet communication, adolescent and Internet Socially Interactive Technologies (SIT's) use and gender differences and Internet communication. The second section includes the review of literature regarding gender differences in mental health and effect of Internet communication on adolescent's mental health. Third section includes the review of studies related to gender differences in psychosocial adjustment and impact of Internet communication on adolescent psychosocial adjustment. The fourth section pertains to the review of literature on gender differences in academic performance followed by a review of studies related to the effect of Internet communication on adolescent academic performance. Last section deals with the review of studies that focus on gender differences in parent-child relationship and influence of Internet communication on adolescent's relationship with their parents.

3.1 ADOLESCENTS AND INTERNET COMMUNICATION

Although social media was fundamentally created for connecting people across the world and allowing them to share their thoughts and opinions. However, it has also led a lot of people to spend too much time in front of the computer, so much so that it becomes the center of their lives. This can lead to an Internet or computer addiction.

Internet-related behavior is often described as Internet addiction, Internet addiction disorder, Internet pathological use, or Internet dependency. The prevalence of Internet addiction varies from 1.5 per cent to 25 per cent in different populations. Surveys have shown a prevalence of 0.3-0.7 per cent in the general population. A recent study reported a prevalence of 0.7 per cent among Indian adolescents.

Internet addiction impairs adolescents 'cognitive function and leads to kinds of maladaptive problems, such as reduced academic achievement, impaired psychological well-being, and increased psychosomatic symptoms and interpersonal problems (Yen et al., 2008; Yuan et al., 2011;Thoméeetal, 2012; Deng and Zhu, 2018).

A study carried out by Pallanti, Bernardi and Quercioli (2006) on a sample of 275 adolescent which consisted of 52.4 per cent males and 47.6 per cent females showed that 5.4 per cent of the sample was Internet addicted. This research also shows that in Italy, Internet usage had a slower diffusion than in other countries. However, a research from China Internet Network Information Center (2006) had shown that 123 million people had gone online, of which 14.9 per cent were teenagers below 18 years old and it has concluded that Internet addiction is currently becoming a serious mental health problem among Chinese adolescents.

Park, Kim and Cho (2008) conducted a study and found that there are more adolescent using the Internet than any other age group in South Korea. Based on their research 97 per cent of South Korean adolescents between the age of 6 and 19 years used the Internet in 2005.

Lin, Lin and Wu (2009) in their respective study showed that older adolescents appear to be more dependent on the Internet than younger adolescent. Studies have found that 19.8 per cent of adolescent in the world have Internet addiction and, furthermore, it is associated with hostility (Ko, Yen, Liu, Huang, and Yen, 2009).

Das & Saboo (2011) reported that the use of Social Network Services (SNSs) have been increasing drastically. It is reported in the Pew Internet and American Life Report (2015)that 95 per cent of American teenagers whose age range from 12 to 17 years old have the accessibility to go online and 80 per cent of the teenagers are users of SNSs (Lenhart, 2011). In addition, the usage of SNSs was so drastic that the teenagers log on to it every day. 46 per cent of teenagers reported that they log in several times a day.

Khan, Khan and Bhatti (2011) investigated the attitudes of students at the Islamia University of Bahawalpur, Pakistan, towards learning through the Internet. Results showed that a vast majority of the students learnt how to use the Internet by themselves or with the assistance of their friends. Their attitude towards the Internet was very positive and they used it mainly for study purposes. They used online databases, dictionaries, encyclopaedias and online courses. Google was the most popular search engine for retrieving information on the Internet. However, the respondents were also dissatisfied with the Internet service provision, slow speed of the Internet connection and inadequate number of computers in computer labs.

Sancheti, (2012) conducted a survey to understand the Internet usage among youngsters. Results revealed the fact that Internet use had both positive and negative impact on the lives of youngsters. Youngsters' face problems like decreased physical activities, decreased time of studies and felt depressed. However, it has positive impact on writing and communication skills. Internet use has major impact on the personal, social and academic life of students. Though students use Internet for learning, surfing academic information, projects/ researches; but the most famous online activities of students is social networking. So, one can understand that Internet is both boon and bane for students (Rangaswamy, 2012).

Chathoth et al., (2014) conducted a cross-sectional comparative study on impact of Internet addiction between addictive Internet users and non-addictive Internet users among undergraduate medical students between the age group of 18 to 20 years. The two groups were compared for environmental stressors and lifestyle factors such as sleep, dietary pattern, physical activity and hobbies. The findings of the study revealed that the addictive Internet user group had a statistically significant impairment of sleep (94.11 per cent Vs 45.2 per cent) and excessive daytime sleepiness (88.23 per cent Vs 39.72 per cent) and presence of environmental stressors (76.47 per cent Vs 36.98 per cent) as compared to non-addictive Internet users

Phong, Srou, and Solá(2016) examined Cambodian phone users' knowledge, attitudes and practices in relation to language reading, writing, and search habits, and identified the factors motivating (and discouraging) their use of Khmer script. The findings showed that almost a third of Cambodians used the Internet to read and write—activities once limited to the classroom or office. This reading and writing activity allows them to access more information, enhance their communication skills, and increase their level of social participation. The significant result of this is that the gender gap in access to information has reduced.

According to Internet and Mobile Association of India (IAMAI, 2018) the world population has ranked India 2nd among the highest number (500 million users till June 2018), approximately 35.5 per cent, of Internet users subsequent to China.

India –Internet Prevalence and Effect

In its International Consortium of Universities for the Study of Biodiversity and the Environment (ICUBE, 2018) report that tracks digital adoption and usage trends in India, it was noted that the number of Internet users in India had registered an annual growth of 18 per cent and was estimated at 566 million as of December 2018. A 40 per cent overall Internet penetration was observed in the report. It projected a double digit growth for 2019 and estimated that the number of Internet users would reach 627 million by the end of this year. Of the total user based, 87 per cent or 493 million Indians were defined as regular users. Nearly 293 million active Internet users reside in urban India, while there were 200 million active users in rural India. The report also noted that the Internet usage was more gender balanced than ever before with women comprising 42 per cent of total Internet users.

Nalwa and Anand (2004) carried out a study among school children of 16-18 years old in India. Two groups were identified dependents and non-dependents. Significant behavioral and functional usage differences were revealed between the two groups. Dependents were found to delay other work to spend time online, lose sleep due to late night logons and felt life would be boring without Internet by dependents than those of non-dependants. On the loneliness measure, significant differences were found between the two groups, with the dependents scoring higher than the non-dependants.

Chandra (2005) reported that the number of Internet users in India had grown five fold since 2005. Mobile Internet usage was growing at the rate of nearly 85 per cent per annum, with nearly 75 per cent of non-voice usage being devoted to entertainment, where video and music streaming were major growth activities. The understanding that the Internet use can be a disorder was still in its initial stages in India. There were limited numbers of studies estimating how common the issue of Internet addiction was in India.

Internet and Mobile Association of India (2013) conducted a study and reported that there has been an explosive growth in the use of Internet not only in India, but also worldwide in the last decade. The population of India is around 1.2 billion as of 2012, of which the number of Internet users (both urban and rural) is around 205 million.

The use of Internet among adolescents was satisfactory but the awareness and knowledge of cybercrime was less (Debarati, Halder and Jaishankar, 2013). They were not aware about privacy matters and plagiarism problems. The study found that students used YouTube and other sites for viewing obscene movies and clippings but at home they did not surf such sites due to the fear of knowing about it by their parents. Most of the students feared from police in doing something illegal on the Internet. The researchers hoped that students would know about the cybercrime issues and it would help them to become good citizens to spread the awareness about the cybercrime in the society.

Another study carried out by Yadav (2013) reported Internet addiction amongst Indian school students. In the study he found that 11.8 per cent students were Internet Addicted. It was predicted by time spent online, usage of social networking sites and chat rooms and also by presence of anxiety and stress.

Anwar (2014) conducted a study on 300 male and female students. It was found that Internet usage among secondary school students had been rising. The result indicated that Internet usage pattern of male students was quite higher than the female students. It was found that average to high use of Internet positively influenced the academic achievements while no use and extremely high usage had a negative impact on academic achievements of the students.

A study was conducted by Habibi (2015) on the relationship of family function with Internet addiction among girl high school students in Malard. The results of study showed that students' Internet addiction increased with enhancement of improper family function. Also, the results of the study showed that with enhancement of unhealthy problem solving in the family, roles and unhealthy responsibilities in the family, unhealthy affective involvement in the family and unhealthy emotional response in the family, students' Internet addiction increased.

Hema and Krishnamacharyulu (2016) reported on changing face of India by rising pace of Internet. The face of the Indian Internet user was changing rapidly. The emergence of India as a developing nation in the new technological era was marked by growing levels of Internet usage. Internet had emerged as a convenient information acquisition tool in this knowledge era. The objective of this study was intended to focus on growth of Internet usage in India, frequency of Internet usage, Internet contribution to GDP, and which factors were contributing more in Internet growth.

Another study was carried out by Chauhan, Buttar and Singh (2017) to find out the level of Internet addiction among adolescents. A cross sectional survey design was used for 52 randomly selected adolescents from private school of Haridwar, Uttarakhand. Data was collected through Kimberly Young's Internet Addiction Scale (1996). Result showed that more than half participants were using facebook (71 per cent) and whatsapp (71 per cent) for the purposes of chatting (92 per cent), regarding Internet addiction more than half 53.8 per cent of the participants had moderate Internet addiction and 7.7 per cent had severe Internet addiction which could possibly affect the physical and mental health of the youngsters.

3.1.1 Gender Differences and Internet Communication

The issue of gender in regard to the question of Internet use and its effects is an important one. Men and women use the Internet differently and engage in different Internet applications. The following section deals with gender differences in Internet addiction, Internet Usage and Internet attitude:

3.1.1.a Internet Addiction

Ozturk (2007) found that Internet is now especially significant risk for 12 to 18 years age group. Researchers have pointed out that adolescent males use Internet more and get addicted more as compared to their female counterparts (Isiklar, 2012). Some contrary findings of other studies on this issue (Brenner, 1997; Akkoyunlu, 2004; Ferraro et al., 2007; Balci and Gülnar, 2009; Orhan and Ceyhan, 2011) found that there were no significant differences in terms of gender.

One of the survey conducted by Sharma & Sharma (2014) on 391 adolescents found that males students were more addicted to the Internet use than female students. Both boys and girls spent 1.29 hours per day on Internet. The study also concluded that Internet addiction was a mounting problems among students particularly of professional courses.

Şaşmaz, Kurt, Yapici and Yazici (2014) investigated the prevalence and risk factors of Internet addiction among high school students. This cross-sectional study Included 1156 students, among whom 609 were male, and 547 were females. The mean age of the students was 16 years. 79 per cent of the students had a computer at home, and 64 per cent had a home

Internet connection. The results revealed that the addiction rate was 9.3 per cent in girls and 20.4 per cent in boys. The prevalence of Internet addiction was high among boys as compared to girls.

Waldo (2014) carried out a study and analyzed correlation between Internet-addiction and adolescents in terms of sex, kind of school and online behavior. Results showed that females were less addicted to Internet than males and students from government schools were less Internet-addicted than private schools.

Alfred (2014) carried out a study on correlates of Internet addiction among adolescents. The study suggested that female users were less addicted to the Internet than male users possibly due to activities and contents online. Also adolescents from private institute had higher risk possibly due to their social status, ease of access and availability of Internet connections. Male adolescents, from private institutes used Internet for surfing and consumed 7+ hours online and were more addicted to the Internet.

Arthanari, Khalique, Ansari, and Faizi (2017) conducted a study to determine the prevalence of Internet addiction among the school-going adolescents of Aligarh and to measure the association of Internet addiction with the socio-demographics of the study. 1020 participants were selected through a multi-stage sampling technique proportional to the number of students in each class. Data Collection was done using a questionnaire that included Young's 20-item Internet Addiction Test (IAT, 1996). The results showed about 35.6 per cent of the students had Internet addiction. Males (40.6 per cent) were significantly more addicted to the Internet than females (30.6 per cent). On bivariate analysis, a higher age group (17-19 years), male gender and Internet access at home were found to have a significantly higher odds' for Internet addiction.

A study by Tran et al (2017) revealed no gender difference in the extent of Internet addiction. Contrary to findings from previous Asian studies, there was no significant difference between the Internet addiction and non-Internet addiction groups in the proportion of gender although previous Asian studies reported that male gender was a risk factor for Internet addiction. Tran et al, (2017) further postulated that online games and pornography were the main reasons contributing to IA in young men. Their findings suggested that young women were equally vulnerable to Internet addiction. This observation could be due to the fact that young men and women tend to be equal in many aspects of life including the access to Internet.

Kumar, Nawaz, Kumar and Yamuna (2017) carried out a cross sectional study over a period of two months among 138 medical students. Data was collected using a predesigned, pretested questionnaire, with questions adapted from Young's Internet addiction questionnaire (1996) to test Internet addiction. The results of the study showed that 30 per cent students had mild Internet addiction and 10 per cent had moderate Internet addiction. Male gender, Internet usage of more than 5 hours per day and expenditure on the monthly Internet pack of more than Rs. 400 were found to be significantly associated with Internet addiction. More than one third of the students, especially males, had Internet addiction.

In a recent study Shao, Zheng, Wang, Liu, Chen and Yao (2018) carried out a meta analysis study among college students in the People's Republic of China on Internet addiction.The overall sample size was 38,245, with 4573 diagnosed with Internet addiction. The detection rate was higher in male students (16 per cent) than female students (8 per cent).

3.1.1.bInternet Usage

Gender differences in adolescent Internet use have also been reported across countries. For instance, males have been found to have a greater amount of frequency and motivation of the Internet use among Romanian and Dutch children (Valkenburg & Soeters, 2001; Durndell & Haag, 2002), American college students (Schumacher & Morahan -Martin, 2001), English secondary school students (Madell & Muncer, 2004), Israeli school students (Nachmias, Mioduster, & Shelma, 2000), North Cyprus adolescents (Bayraktar & Gun, 2007), Greek adolescent students (Siomos, Dafouli, Braimiotis, Mouzas, & Angelopoulos, 2008), and Hong Kong adolescents (Ho, & Lee, 2001), as well as Korean adult users (Rhee & Kim, 2004).

Young (1998) conducted a comparative study and found that men tend to seek out dominant activities or content online. Those interactive online games that rely particularly on power, dominance, control, and/or violence attract more men than women. Women, on the other hand, seek out close friendships and prefer anonymous communication in which they can hide their appearances. Virtual communities give women a sense of belonging and the ability to share their feelings and emotions in private and convenient ways. Whereas men tend to explore sexual fantasies online, women tend to look for romance in cyberspace.

Significant gender differences in the Internet usage have been reported by Weiser (2000). He reported that males tend to be more familiar with the computers and the Internet as compared to females. Similar results were reported by Morahan-Martin and Schumacher (2000) that males were more likely to be pathological Internet users than females.

Schumacher & Morahan-Martin (2001) conducted a study and found that the culture of the Internet was decidedly masculine at first, so it is no surprise that researchers initially assumed that there would be gender differences in amount and type of Internet usage, based on earlier studies showing that boys spent more time than girls playing video and computer games. Boys were expected to gravitate to online game sites and girls to activities that involved social interaction.

The Pew Internet and American Life Project (2002) noted that in contrast to males, females were more likely to use the Internet to maintain social contacts (Howard 2001). Internet activities are commonly grouped into three general areas like communication, entertainment, and information-gathering, with females often associated with the first and males with the latter two (Shaw & Gant, 2002).

Mediamark Research (2005) had reported that boys (28.9 per cent) were more likely to play games than were girls (11.1per cent). Besides that Griffiths, Davies, and Chappell (2004) also support that boy tended to play games more often than did girls (as cited in Lin & Yu, 2008). As previously stated, researchers have found that male and females use Internet differently, and according to The Pew Internet and American Life (2005), men are more likely than women to use the Internet for information gathering while women more likelyto use it for communication purposes (as cited in McMahan 2005).

Higher use of the Internet for non-communication activities was linked to a modest increase in depressive symptoms (Lenhart and Madden 2007). Interestingly, however, the study found a significant gender difference regarding Internet use and symptoms of depression among the subjects. For males, an increase in the number of hours spent writing and reading e-mail led to larger declines in depression than it did for females. The study further found gender differences in use of social networking sites, especially among older adolescents (age 15-17). In that age group, 70 per cent of girls reported using SNS compared to 54 per cent of boys, and girls were more likely to use the sites to interact with friends. Older adolescent boys, on the other hand, were found to be more than twice as likely as girls their age to use SNS to flirt or to meet new friends. Students frequently became engrossed in computer games due to stress related to worries about school achievement (Kimet al., 2010).

Jones et al. (2009) claimed that males were more frequent Internet users and consequently their usage of e -commerce sites was also very high. Bae and Lee (2011) reported in their study that women attached more risk to online shopping and were more concerned with privacy issues. They further stated that females while making online purchase decisions were more affected by online consumer reviews than males. They have also found that in comparison to males, females were more affected by the negative consumer reviews given online.

Karacic and Oreskovic (2017) conducted a study to identify possible differences in the purpose of Internet use among adolescents with respect to age group, country of residence, and gender and the distribution of Internet addiction across age groups. Another aim was to determine if there is a correlation between the purpose of Internet use and age and if this interaction influences the level of addiction to the Internet. The study included a simple random sample of 1059 adolescents (534 boys and 525 girls) aged 11-18 years attending elementary and grammar schools in Croatia, Finland, and Poland. It was found that adolescents mostly used the Internet for entertainment. More female than male adolescents used it for school work. Internet for the purpose of school/work was mostly used by Polish adolescents followed by Croatian and Finnish adolescents. The level of Internet addiction was the highest among the 15-16 year-old age group and was lowest in the 11-12 year-old age group.

3.1.1.c Internet Attitude

Young (2000) conducted a study in which a survey of students' attitude of computers was developed and used to explore differences in attitude towards computers among middle and high school students. The study indicated that gender differences in attitude resulted from a greater confidence among males about the information technology and the perception amongst females of computers as a male domain and hence a rejection of computers by them.

Lenhart (2005) carried out a study and found that there were also ongoing differences in attitudes about Internet use (excepting e-mail usage) between male and female students. Male students tended to use the Internet more often and to have more positive attitudes than did female students about their experiences online.

Rees and Noyes (2007) found significant gender differences that were reported for computer and Internet use, Internet attitudes, and computer anxiety. Although males and females both were using the technologies, but females were less frequent user of technology as compared to males. Females had less positive attitude and greater anxiety toward technology.

Vijayalakshmi (2014) conducted a study on social networking sites among Indian teenagers. Sites like Facebook, WhatsApp and Twitter are becoming popular and a vital part of social life in India, especially among teenagers. The findings indicated that both boys and girls used other forms of communication channels to strengthen existing friendships more with the same gender than with the opposite. However, the boys enjoyed more freedom when compared with the girls and they admitted talking to online friends and meeting them outside cyberspace without any hesitation. The girls, on their part, were hesitant to extend online friendships beyond virtual space because of security issues and resistance from family members.

From the above review of literature, it is evident that the role of technology is neither good nor bad, it is neutral. It is used as a force to generate energy in society. Nevertheless, Internet communication is the product of technological development. Social networking has become so predominant in people's lives because we all are living in "Network Society". Peoplearein touch with the world constantly. Although, a massive literature has been generated on Cyber-crime and Social networking sites, still ambiguity persists on the impact of technology and social networking sites on society because still the effect is in the infancy stage and much needs to be done. Indian society has a dearth of relevant literature on cyber-crime and social networking sites. It is also noted that very few studies have been conducted and reviewed on adolescents' use of social networking sites in Indian context. The studies which are conducted on the effects of these sites on adolescents provide a mixed stand.

Based on the findings of the above studies it was hypothesized that:

1(a) **Adolescent boys will score significantly higher in terms of Internet Addiction, Internet Usage and Internet Attitude as compared to adolescent girls.**

3.2 MENTAL HEALTH

Mental health has become a priority in public health policy. In 2013 a World Health Assembly resolution was passed by the World Health Organization (WHO) that called for a comprehensive mental health action plan at the national level. In this regard, late adolescents and young adults deserve special attention. Half of all mental health disorders in adulthood start by the age of 14 and three-quarter by the age of 25. Most mental disorders begin during adolescence and early adulthood (10–24 years of age) and poor mental health is associated with negative educational, health and social outcomes (Patel, Flisher, Hetrick, & McGorry, 2007). According to the statistics, in any given year 20 per cent of adolescents worldwide experience mental disorders, most commonly anxiety or depression (WHO, 2012). Mental health problems are considered to be some of the most common and yet most stigmatizing of conditions.

3.2.1 Gender Differences in Mental Health

A study conducted on the mental health as a correlate of intelligence, academic achievement and socioeconomic status by Mangotra (1982) reported that girls appeared to possess better mental health, were capable of facing the realities around them and in a position to tide over the mental health disequilibrium. The mental health of boys and girls appeared to be considerably influenced by the two factors, namely, intelligence and physical health. The mental health of boys was dominated by the feeling of depression and neurotic behavior. On the other hand, girls were found to be suffering from a sense of insecurity and anxiety.

Thayer et al. (1994) found that women rely on social support more frequently to overcome negative moods. Similarly, Tkach and Lyubomirsky (2006), although, found that men and women were equally happy, they uncovered gender differences in the use of happiness-enhancing strategies. These differences can also be attributed to the different domains of life satisfaction. Girls were more satisfied than boys in learning and family and friends, and the opposite was true in physical activities, culminating in no significant difference in overall life satisfaction (Casas et al. 2007).

A study was carried out by Manjuvani (1995) on sex, type of school, standard and mental health status of high school students. Her findings were that girls had better mental health status as compared to boys and mental health status of 10th standard students was low as compared to the 9th standard students.

Harrington (1998) found that even relatively mild depressive symptoms can result in impaired functioning. Female students felt more depression as compared to males (Piccinelli & Wilkinson, 2000; Essau & Petermann, 2000; Ganguli2003; Black, Nair, Paul & John, 2004; Mohanraj & Sub-baiah, 2010; Roberts & Li-Leng, 2012; Verma, Jain & Roy, 2014)

A study on anxiety, depression and coping strategies among adolescents was conducted by Bryme (2000).Results suggested that males present significant decrease of anxiety and fear instead of girls who showed increased in anxiety and both males and females used different coping strategies in order to deal with fear and anxiety.

Extensive study was conducted by Nanda (2001) on the mental health of high school students. The sample consisted of 1579 students from 86 schools. The results revealed that female students were found to have better mental health than male students. While comparing male and female students in urban, rural and ashram schools separately, it was found that male and female students in urban and ashram schools had similar mental health, whereas female students had significantly better mental health than male students in rural schools.

Dost (2007) reported differences between males and females regarding their satisfaction with life. A significant number of studies have also reported higher life satisfaction among males (Goldbeck, Schmitz, Besier, Herschbach, & Henrich, 2007).

Sigfusdottir, Asgeirsdottir, Sigurdssonand Gudjonsson (2008) conducted alongitudinal cross-sectional population based study to examine trends in adolescent depression and anxiety symptoms from 1997 to 2006, using four time-points (1997, 2000, 2003, and 2006), and adolescent mental health service use in the same period, using three time-points (1997, 2000, and 2006). Samples were 14 and 15 year old students, attending the compulsory 9th and 10th grades of the Icelandic secondary school system. They completed questionnaires related to mental health. In total, 21,245 students participated in the four studies. The findings showed symptoms of depression among girls. Anxiety among both boys and girls had increased among the selected sample of adolescents in Iceland. The study concluded that more attention has to be given to adolescent girls because of the increasing risk for depression and anxiety symptoms.

A prospective study was carried out by Chaplin and Gillham et al (2009) to examine gender differences in the relationship between anxiety and depressive symptoms in early adolescence. The sample comprised of 113 students in the age range of 11 to 14 years. A questionnaire was administered to this student which assesses the depressive symptoms at an initial assessment and 1 year later. Total anxiety, worry and oversensitivity symptoms were found to predict later depressive symptoms more strongly for girls than for boys. Physiological anxiety predicted later depressive symptoms for both boys and girls. These findings highlight the importance of anxiety for the development of depression in adolescence, particularly worry and oversensitivity among girls.

One of the studies was carried out on personality development of adolescents by Sravanthi, Devi and Saroda (2009). The sample comprised of 180 students (90 boys and 90 girls). Multi Dimensional Assessment of Personality Series(MAPS) teenage form covering 20 dimensions was used for data collection. The mental health dimension revealed that majority of boys and girls (44 per cent) fell into average category followed by 39 per cent in high category and 17 per cent in low category. It also indicated that mental health of adolescent boys was better than those of girls.

Khasakhala et al (2012) conducted a cross-sectional study to determine the prevalence of depressive symptoms among adolescents in Nairobi (Kenya) public secondary schools. A random sample of school going adolescents (n=1276) were taken from 17 secondary schools. Results revealed that the prevalence of clinically significant depressive symptoms was 26.4 per cent and the occurrence was higher in girls than in boys. Students in boarding schools had more clinically significant depressive symptoms than day scholars.

Bandhana, Darshana and Sharma (2012) found significant relationship between home environment, mental health and academic achievement among higher secondary school students. Home environment and mental health had significantly contributed to the academic achievement of 12th grade higher secondary school students. The mean value of mental health of girls was significantly more compared to boys.

To investigate the relationship between age, depression and academic performance among adolescents, Busari (2012) carried out a study among 1200 students (600 male and 600 female) in the age range 15-19 years. The results showed that 26.5 per cent of the boys and 30.7 per cent of the girls were depressed indicating that girls were more depressed than boys.

Dahlen, Steffenak and Thander (2017) conducted a study on adolescents (n=8052) from secondary school grades 8, 9 and 10 (age 13–16 years) from 41 municipal schools in four counties.The aim of this study was to compare and describe gender differences and the associations between symptoms of depression and family conflict and economics, lifestyle habits, school satisfaction and the use of health-care services among adolescents. Results showed that girls reported a higher prevalence of symptoms of depression than boys. Gender differences were seen on all items related to symptoms of depression, family conflict and economics, lifestyle habits, school satisfaction and health-care services. Multiple regressions showed that family conflicts and economics contributed to 19.2 per cent of the variance in symptoms of depression in girls and 12.4 per cent in boys. School satisfaction made a strong contribution: 21.5 per cent in girls and 15.4 per cent in boys. The total model explained 49 per cent of the total variance in symptoms of depression in girls and 32.5 per cent in boys.

Based on the findings of the above studies it was hypothesized that:

1(b) **Adolescent girls will score significantly higher in terms of Depression, General Positive Affect, Emotional Ties and Life Satisfaction as compared to adolescent boys.**

1(c) **Adolescent boys will score significantly higher in terms of Anxiety and Loss of Behavioural/Emotional Control as compared to adolescent girls.**

3.2.2 Internet Communication and Mental Health

The Internet is a new tool that is evolving into an essential part of everyday life all over the world and its use has increased especially among young people. In spite of the widely perceived merits of this tool, psychologists and educators have been aware of the negative impacts of its use, especially the over or misuse and the related physical and psychological problem is Internet addiction (Murali & George, 2007). The problem of Internet addiction is a raising phenomenon affecting people with varying frequency around the world and has produced negative impacts on the academic, relationship, financial, and occupational aspects of many lives (Chou & Hsiao, 2000).

Users who spend a significant amount of time online often experience academic, relationship, financial, and occupational difficulties, (Murphey, 1996; Scheres, 1997) as well as physical impairments (Chou, 2005). Some researchers (Brenner, 1997; Nie & Erbring, 2000) have even linked Internet use with an increase in psychological difficulties such as depression, loneliness (Young & Rodger, 1998; Krant et al, 2002) and frustration (Clark et al, 2004).

Young (1996) conducted a study and reported a link between Internet Addiction Disorder with existing mental health issues, most commonly depression. Young stated that the disorder had significant effects socially, psychologically and occupationally. Addicts were found to use the Internet on an average of 38 hours a week for non-academic and non-employment purposes resulting in poor grades among students, discord among couples and reduced work performance. Many of these characteristics were the same ones that have been shown to put individuals at high risk for other psychological problems or disorders such as depression (Young, 1998).

In one of the study Kandell (1998) reported that there were a number of emotional factors which may be related to college students' Internet addiction. Among these factors the most remarkable were depression, anxiety, and stress. Research on Internet addiction and depression demonstrated that the overuse of the Internet, which results in a disruption of the normal life of an individual and the people around him, was associated with an increase in the frequency of depression (Erbring, 2002). Because, excessive Internet use can displace valuable time that people spend with family and friends and which eventually leads to smaller social circles and higher levels of loneliness and stress (Nie et al., 2002). Other conclusions of excessive usage have been documented as neglect of academic work, domestic responsibilities, disruption of relationships, social isolation, and financial problems (Griffiths, 2000; McKenna &Bargh, 2000).

Kraut and his colleagues (1998) investigated the impact of Internet on individuals and they argued that greater use of the Internet was associated with negative effects on individuals, like a diminishing social circle, and increasing depression and loneliness.

Some of the specific researches conducted in this area include Shapira (2000), who found that all 20 individuals identified as having Internet addiction also had at least one lifetime DSM-IV Axis 1 diagnosis. In another study, Black (1999) found that nearly 50 per cent of participants who reported compulsive computer use also met the diagnostic criteria for a psychological disorder, with the most commonly reported disorders being substance use (38 per cent), mood disorder (33 per cent), and anxiety disorder (19 per cent). Young (1998) found that 54 per cent of individuals identified as having Internet addiction also had diagnoses of depression and 34 per cent had anxiety disorders. This was validated in a study among Beijing high school students that found that online game addiction was significantly correlated to depression (Qin, Rao &Zhong, 2007).

Rainie and Kohut (2000 a) identified significant relationships between the degree of psychiatric symptoms and the severity of Internet addiction. Addicted Internet use was significantly correlated with psychiatric symptoms. Psychologists and educators are aware of the potential negative impact of addicted use and related physical and psychological problems. Users who spend a significant amount of time online often experience academic, relational, economic, and occupational problems, as well as physical disorders. Internet use was significantly correlated with psychiatric symptoms.

In yet another study by Rainie andKohut (2000b), the results revealed that student who used Internet six hours a day generally reported more psychiatric symptoms. Addicted and non-addicted Internet users displayed significant difference on interpersonal relationships. Individuals with Internet addiction experienced a sense of criticism by others, coyness and a sense of uneasiness against gender.

Beard and Wolf (2001) found that Internet addiction can affect people of any gender, age, and socioeconomic status. The sense of satisfaction that comes along the Internet indulgences feeds a negative cycle where more time spent online means less real social contact and less physical activity, increasing the vulnerability to psychological disorders.

Engelberg and Sjoberg (2004) showed that students who used Internet six hours a day generally reported more psychiatric symptoms, compared to students who did not. The main goal of their study was to investigate the relationships between addicted Internet and Psychiatric Symptoms. The study found significant relationships between the daily Internet use and the degree of psychiatric symptoms such as depression, obsessive compulsion, interpersonal sensitivity, anxiety, hostility, phobic anxiety, paranoid ideation and psychoticism.

One of the similar findings was being reported by Ko, Yen, and Chen (2005) that Internet addiction also may contribute to anxiety and stress. Those who suffered from anxiety and stress often have a great deal of trouble communicating and interacting with others in a healthy, positive, and meaningful way. These human characteristics were viewed as important determinants of Internet addiction.

Ha (2007) evaluated the relationship between depression and Internet addiction among adolescents. A total of 452 Korean adolescents were studied. First, they were evaluated for their severity of Internet addiction with consideration of their behavioral characteristics and their primary purpose for computer use. Second, the researchers investigated correlations between Internet addiction and depression, alcohol dependence and obsessive-compulsive symptoms. Internet addiction was significantly associated with depressive symptoms and obsessive-compulsive symptoms.

Studies conducted by Shaw and Black (2008)andTao (2010)reported thatInternet addiction was typically characterized by psychomotor agitation, anxiety, craving, depression, hostility, substance experience preoccupation, loss of control, withdrawal, impairment of function, reduced decision-making ability and constant online surfing despite negative effects on social and psychological welfare.

Mitchel (2008) found that excessive use of the Internet among students lead to physical and psychological problems, their happiness and positive thoughts were reduced and they had academic problems. The study of Dehghani (2009) showed that addicts used the Internet more often when they were depressed than non-addicts.

Tsai et al, (2009) reported that the risk of excessive Internet usage was high in depressed individuals. Depression is related to disabilities, tension, fatigue, lack of patience, failure to perform tasks, and Internet Addiction. People tend to engage in addictive behaviour in order to control depression and anxiety while reflecting their internal emptiness or sense of anxiety (Kimet al., 2006). In addition, in cases of Internet Addiction, real-life relationships deteriorate, and the sufferer becomes more socially isolated as his/her Internet usage time increases. Such isolation further absorbs adolescents into the Internet, because it makes them even more depressed (Young & Rogers, 1998).

Van Den Eijunden,& Van De Mheen (2010) conducted a study and found that depression, loneliness, and low self-esteem have been associated with excessive online gaming in Dutch adolescents between the ages of 13 and 16. Correlation between depression and Internet addiction was also observed in Turkish high school students (Üneri & Tanidir, 2011).

Shahbazzadegan (2011) in his research showed that there was a significant difference between Internet users and non-users in mental health and aggression. Internet addicted showed an increase in psychological difficulties such as depression and loneliness. Addicted users were more probable to be depressed than non-addicted Internet users.

Akin and Iskender (2011) conducted a study to examine the relationships between Internet addiction, depression, anxiety, and stress. Participants were 300 university students in Turkey. Internet addiction was found positively related to depression, anxiety, and stress. According to path analysis results, depression, anxiety, and stress were predicted positively by Internet addiction. This research showed that Internet addiction has a direct impact on depression, anxiety, and stress.

Bhadauria, Gore and Pandey (2011) studied the effect of excessive use of Internet upon adolescent's mental health. In this study adolescent between age group of 17-18 years were selected from Class XI of senior secondary school of Banda city. The major findings of the study were that Internet usage negatively affected the mental health of adolescents.

Ali, Razieh, Zaman, and Narjesskhatoon (2012) investigated the prevalence of Internet addiction among university students and the relationship between Internet addiction with anxiety. Participants were 330 students who were randomly selected from different universities. The results of this study demonstrated that prevalence of Internet addiction among boys was more than girls. The addiction to Internet was more among science and engineering students than art and humanity students. There was a significant difference in four groups in anxiety levels. The result of regression analysis showed that anxiety and sex could significantly predict Internet addiction.

A study was conducted by Yadav, Banwari, Parmar, and Maniar (2013)on Internet addiction and its correlates among high school students ofAhmedabad, India. This was one of the first such effort to study Internet Addiction amongst Indian school students of class 11th and 12th and to find its correlation with socio-educational characteristics, Internet use patterns and psychological variables, namely depression, anxiety and stress. Six hundred and twenty one students of six English medium schools of Ahmadabad participated, of which 552 (88.9 per cent) who completed forms were analysed. Sixty-five (11.8 per cent) students had Internet Addiction; it was predicted by time spent online, usage of social networking sites and chat rooms, and also by presence of anxiety and stress. There was a strong positive correlation between Internet Addiction and depression, anxiety and stress.

Liu (2014) studied the long term effects of heavy use of video on health, mental health and education among adolescents in the U.S. It was found that it leads to behavioral problem for users, such as academic failure, physical and mental health problems.

Azher et al. (2014) conducted a study on the prevalence of Internet addiction among the male and female students at the University of Sargodha and the relationship between Internet addiction and anxiety level of these students. The results showed that prevalence of Internet was more among male students than female students. Regression analysis showed a positive and significant relation between Internet addiction and anxiety level among University students.

Morsunbul (2014) analyzed the relationship between life satisfaction and Internetaddiction, he observed that individuals with higher life satisfaction had less Internet addiction.

Okwarajiet et al. (2015) examined gender differences, Internet addiction and psychological distress among adolescents. This study was carried out in Enugu, south east Nigeria and found that adolescents exhibited presence of Internet addiction and psychological distress.

Karacicand Oreskovic (2017) conducted a study on the influence of Internet addiction of adolescents in Croatia and Germany and its impact on the subjective feeling of health status. There is a strong correlation between adolescents' mental health and quality of life and the level of their Internet addiction. Out of the total number of adolescents who had ill-health, 39 per cent of them were moderately addicted to the Internet. Out of the total number of adolescents 20 per cent in medium health were problematically addicted to the Internet. Finally, out of the total number of adolescents in good health 13 per cent were highly addicted to the Internet. Therefore, higher Internet addiction leads to poor health among adolescents.

Another recent study was conducted by Cherian (2018) on Internet addiction among university engineering students and its association with psychological distress and its impact on their educational progress, academic competence, and long-term career goals. This study was a first such attempt to explore Internet use behaviors, Internet Addiction, among a large group of engineering students from India, and its association with psychological distress primarily depressive symptoms. One thousand eighty six engineering students aged 18–21 years pursuing bachelors in engineering from the south Indian city of Mangalore participated in the study. The results showed thatout of the total of 1086, students 27.1 per cent of engineering students met criterion for mild addictive Internet use, 9.7 per cent for moderate addictive Internet use, and 0.4 per cent for severe addiction to Internet. IA was higher among engineering students who were male, staying in rented accommodations, accessed Internet several times a day, spent more than 3 h per day on Internet, and had psychological distress. Gender, duration of use, time spent per day, frequency of Internet use, and psychological distress (depressive symptoms) predicted Internet Addiction. The study showed that a substantial proportion of engineering students have Internet Addiction.

In a very recent study Sharma and Sharma (2018) investigated the Internet addiction and psychological well-being among college students. The study was conducted with the objective to find out the relationship between Internet addiction and Psychological Well Being (PWB) of college students. The result showed that Internet addiction was significantly and negatively correlated to PWB and sub dimensions of PWB. Hence, the researchers argued that it is important to develop various policies for the prevention of Internet addiction which is very essential for promoting PWB of college students.

Based on the review of the findings of the above studies it was hypothesized that:

2(a) **Internet Addiction will be significantly and positively related to Anxiety, Depression, Loss of Behavioral /Emotional Control among adolescent boys.**

2(b) **Internet Addiction will be significantly and negatively related to General Positive Affect, Emotional Ties and Life Satisfaction among adolescent boys.**

2(c) **Internet Addiction will be significantly and positively related to Anxiety, Depression, and Loss of Behavioral /Emotional Control among adolescent girls.**

2(d) **Internet Addiction will be significantly and negatively related to General Positive Affect, Emotional Ties and Life Satisfaction among adolescent girls.**

2(e) **Internet Usage will be significantly and positively related to Anxiety and Depression among adolescent boys.**

2(f) **Internet Usage will be significantly and positively related to Anxiety and Depression among adolescent girls**

3.3PSYCHOSOCIAL ADJUSTMENT

Psychosocial adjustment has been considered as one of the major contributing psychological factor in characterizing the individuals. The adolescents have to develop the adjustment ability which in turn will make them grow as responsible citizens of the society.

3.3.1 Gender Differences and Psychosocial Adjustment

Anita (1994) provided an insight into the gender differences in adolescents self-concept and adjustment. It was depicted from the results that girls were better adjusted in emotional, social, educational areas of adjustment as compared to boys.

Prabha & Krishna (1998) conducted a comparative study on 240 adolescent girls and boys of employed and non-employed mothers in age group 14-18 years on school adjustment. The objective was to study the difference between boys and girls in their emotional, social and educational sphere of school adjustment. The study revealed that there was a significant difference in total adjustment between boys and girls. Girls showed better adjustment than boys.

In order to investigate the adjustment problems of intermediate students Mythili (2004) selected a sample of 150 boys and girls students randomly from government and private management colleges in Vijayawada. A Telugu version of the Mooney problem checklist was administered. The results reported that boys had more adjustment problems as compared to girls.

Sharma (2005) conducted a study on the adjustment problem of adolescent students in relation to their sex. The findings of the study revealed that the majority of the adolescenthad family, school, social and personal adjustment problems. Both male and female students did not differ from each other on family, personal and total adjustment. Male students had more school and social adjustment problems in comparison to female students.

The school adjustment of 60 rural adolescents with reference to their emotional and social sphere was assessed and compared by Shalu and Audichya (2006). The sample consisted of 30 rural boys and 30 rural girls between the age group of 15-18 years studying in government co-educational school only. The Adjustment Inventory for school students constructed by Sinha and Singh (1984) which was modified by the investigator, was used for data collection. They reported significant gender difference in social and emotional adjustment. Rahamtullah (2007) stated that boys were significantly better adjusted than girls on the emotional adjustment area.

A study was conducted on adjustment problems of adolescent student by Talukdar, Nurayan and Chaliha (2008). The objective of the study was to find out the level of adjustment of male and female adolescent student in the areas namely home, health, social, emotional and educational and to find out major factors leading to adjustment problems of male and female adolescent student. The result of the study revealed that the home, health, social and educational adjustment of male student was found to be average. Male students' emotional adjustment was not satisfactory.

Gupta and Gupta (2011) found that female children were better in social adjustment while in educational adjustment boys and girls had same order of adjustment.

A study on the social, emotional and educational problems of adolescents in relation to their personality factors was carried out by Baroowa (2012). The sample of the study was 150 boy and 150 girl students of class XI and class XII of greater Guwahati city. The findings indicated that girls had more social problems than boys. In case of emotional adjustment area it was found that 40 per cent of the students were in the good category of adjustment which indicates that adolescents were emotionally more or less stable. It was found that girls were more emotionally stable then the boys.

Chauhan (2013) conducted a study on adjustment of higher secondary school students of Durg district and results indicated that there is significant difference in adjustment of higher secondary school students and female students had good adjustment level as compared to the male students.

In order to studyadjustment and academic achievement of higher secondary school students research was carried out by Mansingbhai & Patel (2013)results revealed that male adolescent differed significantly on health, social and emotional adjustment as compared to female adolescent.

While examining adjustment of adolescent boys and girls in Ahmadabad Vishal & Kaji (2014) selected a sample size of 120 boys and girls. The result showed that there was a significant difference in home, social and emotional adjustment of boys and girls. The girls were highly adjusted in social and emotional areas of adjustment than the boys. Home adjustment was higher among boys than the girls. Findings showed that there was no significant difference between school adjustments of the school students in relation to gender.

Panth, Chaurasia & Gupta (2015) investigated a comparative study of adjustment and emotional maturity between gender and stream of undergraduate students and results revealed that the level of emotional maturity and adjustment of girls was higher than boys.

With the purpose to compare emotional adjustment of secondary school students in relation to their gender, academic achievement and parent-child relationship Bhagat (2016) conducted a studyon a sample of 200 randomly selected secondary school students of 9th class studying in government and private schools of Samba District (J&K). The results of the study showed that female secondary school students were emotionally more adjusted as compared to male secondary school students. The high achiever secondary school students were emotionally more adjusted as compared to low achiever secondary school students who had a better relationship with their parents were emotionally more adjusted as compared to who had low parent-child relationship.

Sarkar and Banik (2017) aimed to investigate the adjustment of adolescent student in West Tripura in relation to their academic achievement, age, gender, etc. The sample size was 120 adolescents (60 boys & 60 girls). The results revealed that there was a significant difference in emotional adjustment, social adjustment, educational adjustment and academic achievement among adolescent boys and girls.

Based on the findings of the above studies it was hypothesized that:

1(d)   Adolescent boys will score significantly higher in terms of Emotional and School Adjustment as compared to adolescent girls.

1(e)   Adolescent girls will score significantly higher in terms of Family, Health and Social Adjustment as compared to adolescent boys.

3.3.2 Internet Communication and Psychosocial Adjustment

Psychosocial denotes the mental and the social factors in a person's life, for instance, relationships, education, age, and employment that pertain to a person's life history (Pugh, 2002). Those who lack confidence in social interaction offline tend to escape to online interactions (Caplan, 2007). When people procrastinate, they become stressed.Some choose to escape from stress by becoming immersed in cyberspace (Buckner, Castille, & Sheets, 2012).

Kraut and Lundmark (1998) reported a causal relationship between increased Internet use and loneliness, depression, and social disconnection among young people. Other studies have reached somewhat similar conclusions (e.g., Nie & Erbring, 2000, Nie, 2001;Beebe, Asche, Harrison, & Quinlan, 2004). However, the bulk of research, including a study by Kraut et al. (2002), has led to a reconceptualization of the psychosocial impact of Internet use.

A study was conducted by Subrahmanyam, Greenfield, Kraut, and Gross (2001) on moderate computer use and they concluded that the use of computer may have prosaically effects on young people, helping them sustain friendships, but they added that there have been relatively few studies on the subject.

Heitner (2002) carried out a study on the relationship of Internet use and social development among adolescents. The study examined separated Internet usage into three categories, not social (mainly playing single-user games and surfing the Web), asynchronous social (e-mail and posting messages), and synchronous social (real-time interactions such as IM, chat rooms, and multi-user online games). Teenagers gravitating to the first two categories were found to have more social skills deficits and lower peer status and to be more socially introverted.In one national survey of adolescents, nearly half of those questioned said the Internet has improved their relationships with their friends (Lenhart et al., 2001).

Nearly all teenagers who use the Internet, they are more likely to be communicating with close friends online than with strangers (Gross, 2004). Supportive relationships with friends have been found to contribute to a young person's sense of well-being, self-esteem, connectedness, and ability to cope with stress (Greenberg, Siegel, & Leitch, 1983; Hartup, 1996).

As has been reported by Rideout, Roberts, and Foehr (2005)that young people on average are exposed to the equivalent of eight hours a day of visual, auditory, and text (electronic and print) media content. Some early research on Internet use (e.g., Kraut, Lundmark, et al., 1998; Nie & Erbring, 2000 and Nie, 2001) raised concerns that teenagers who spent a lot of time online might be prone to social isolation, loneliness, depression, and reduced psychological well-being. McKenna and Bargh (2000) noted that the initial apprehension about the impact of the Internet was similar to that which greeted the advent of the telephone and television. They asserted that situational and personal variables were more salient than the amount of time spent online, because people used the Internet for a variety of reasons and motivations and it had different effects on them accordingly.

Al-Ausaimi (2010) carried out a study in which they targeted at recognizing the relationship between Internet addiction and psychosocial adjustment on a sample of 350 students from Kingdom of Saudi Arabia. The results revealed a statistically significant negative correlation between scores of the Internet addiction scale and scores of psychosocial adjustment indicating that higher addiction to Internet lowered the psychosocial adjustment of the students.

One of the studies conducted by Sharma and Anu (2014) which examined influence of Internet-addiction on mental health and adjustment of college students. Results revealed that excessive use of Internet leads the students to decreased mental health and adjustment level among college students. So, the researchers concluded that Internet addiction, mental health and adjustment are closely related to each other.

Yousef and Atoum (2015) carried out a study on Internet addiction and its relation to psychosocial adaptation among Jordanian High School Students. In their respective study they tried to identify the stages of Internet needs between high school students (8th, 9th and 10th grades). They also found effect of mental problems and other variables which were related to Internet use and depended on Internet addiction. They also found that the Internet was attractive, and because of that so many users suffer problems in psychosocial adaptation. It was one of the correlated factors with isolation, anxiety, depression, difficulty of focus and social problems in general. Study also suggested that depression, distraction, over activity, social anxiety, self-esteem and power of motivation were the most predicting variables of Internet addiction.

Based on the findings of the above studies it was hypothesized that:

3(a)   **Internet Addiction will be significantly and positively related to Emotional, Family, Health, Social and School Adjustment of adolescent boys.**

3(b)   **Internet Addiction will be significantly and positively related to Emotional, Family, Health, Social and School adjustment of adolescent girls.**

3.4 ACADEMIC PERFORMANCE

The academic performance of every individual is not equal. There is a lot of variability and dispersion. The variability cannot be attributed to a single factor, but it is the outcome of a number of factors such as intelligence, study habits, self-concept, creativity, aptitude, interests, socio economic factors, area etc.

3.4.1 Gender Differences in Academic Performance

Along with the above mentioned factors gender of the child is also an influencing factor on academic achievement of the child (Abdullahi and Bitchi, 2015). The relationship between gender and the academic achievement of students has been discussed for decades (Eitle, 2005). A gap between the achievement of adolescent boys and girls has been found, with girls showing better performance than boys in certain instances (Chambers and Schreiber, 2004).

While conducting a comparative study on intelligence and academic achievement of adolescent boys and girls of IX and XI class Diseth (2003) found that among students of class XI there was no difference in the academic achievement of intellectually superior and intellectually very superior boys and girls. At other intellectual levels the academic achievement of girls was superior to that of boys. In general the intelligence test scores of boys were higher than those for the girls. In case of boys there was very high correlation between intelligence test scores and academic achievement whereas in case of girls there was average correlation.

In order to study and explore the relationships between academic achievement, demographic and psychological factors Bruni (2006) carried out a study on a sample of 380 school students of Italy. School Achievement Index was used as an instrument to measure their academic achievement. The findings of the study indicated significant difference in academic achievement of male and female students. Female students were found to have higher academic achievement than males.

A study was done on the impact of motivation on academic achievement in Mathematics by Tella (2007). The participants of the study were 450 secondary school students of both sexes drawn from ten schools of Ibadan. Data was collected by employing achievement test in mathematics as a measure of academic achievement. The results revealed significant differences in the academic achievement of male and female students in mathematics. Male students were found to have better achievement in mathematics.

Asthana (2011) conducted a study on a sample of 300 students consisting 150 male and 150 female students of secondary education from Varanasi, with a view to assess the gender difference in scholastic achievement. Scholastic achievement was measured on the basis of an average of marks obtained in three previous annual examinations. The findings revealed that there was a significant difference in academic achievement of male and female students. Girls were found to be better performers than boys.

A study was carried out by Sood (2012)on need for achievement, academic achievement and socio-demographic variables of high school students of Kullu and Manali districts of Himachal Pradesh. The results revealed that need for achievement positively and significantly affected academic achievement of high school students. The students with high n-achievement possessed significantly higher academic achievement as compared to students with average and low n-achievement. Girls were found to have significantly higher n-achievement in comparison to boys. However, no significant differences in n-achievement were found among rural and urban students as well as students belonging to nuclear and joint families.

Recently, Gutierrez, LAgudo, and García (2018) reported that adolescents show gender differences in academic performance. It was observed that girls were less likely to get low scores than boys. More interestingly, gender differences in the returns to expectations about the future had been found to explain most of this advantage for girls, while boys relied more on their initial learning skills to pass. Additionally, it was found that boys were more prone to behavioral problems than girls, whereas boys' academic results were more sensitive to changes with their family's socio-economic status, which also explained a significant portion of the gender differences in academic achievement.

In yet another recent study Patiyal, Choudhary, and Mehta (2018) carried out a research on 500 school going students of CBSE and MP Board. The samples were selected by random sampling method. The aim of the study was to assess the gender differences in academic performance of boys and girls in relation to mental health. The boys, girls and students of CBSE with higher mental health had better academic performance than other groups with those of lower mental health of MP Board having lowest academic performance.

Hence, it could be concluded that the gender influences academic success of the students at all levels of education. Gender, locale and parental education have direct influence on the academic achievement of the students.

Based on the review of the above studies it was hypothesized that:

1(f)   Adolescent girls will score significantly higher in terms of Academic Performance as compared to adolescent boys.

3.4.2Internet Communication and Academic Performance

With the increasing global penetration of the Internet, concerns have been expressed that some people may over–use the technology to such an extent that their behavior might be considered pathological. For example, because of their over–engagement in Internet–related activities, children and adolescents have been shown to suffer from academic failure, difficulty in completing class assignments, lack of attentiveness in class, sleep deprivation, and depression (Douglas, 2008).

Bremer, Rauch and Tapscott (1998) and Papadakis (2001) found in their respective studies that the Internet, with its global reach, has generally been considered a resource that can enhance a young person's academic as well as social development. Nearly all teenagers who go online report using the Internet for school research, and nearly 90 per cent of parents believe that Internet helps their children with academics (Lenhart et al., 2001). In another national study, more than 60 per cent of students aged 18 and under stated that the Internet was very important or extremely important in doing their schoolwork (USC Annenberg School Center for the Digital Future, 2004).In the same survey, nearly 80 per cent of parents said that Internet access at home had produced no change in their children's grades.

A study was carried out by Anderson (2000) on Internet addiction and patterns of its use among college students. The sample size was 1302 students. The results revealed that about 10 per cent of the students, mostly males, were Internet addicts who face difficulties in their scientific and academic lives in addition to different patterns of sleeping.

In research involving high school students in California, users of MySpace reported their grades had declined significantly over the past year (Research links MySpace, 2007). Factors relating to adolescent use of the Internet and messaging media had an impact on academic performance. It was reported that many students had the ability to send text messages or instant messaging during class time at school, perhaps detracting them from their attention to what is being taught. At home, many teenagers had access to a range of media equipment in their bedrooms: 68 per cent had TV and 31 per cent had computers where supervision by adults was less likely (Rideout, 2005).

It was reported by Kumar and Kaur (2006) in their study that the students found Internet information more valuable and it helped them to improve their academic competence. Due to the update and instant availability of information, their dependency on Internet had increased and they felt that the Internet had improved their professional aptitude. On the other hand, some students also claimed that, no doubt, Internet had revolutionised their life but it could not replace library.

Jang, Hwang and Choi (2008) conducted a study and observed the severity, cause, and symptoms of Internet addiction of emerging importance for educators. If digital games are used for a long time or without a clear purpose, instructors may be unintentionally contributing to learners' Internet addiction (Liu, 2011). Similar expectations are applicable to college level educators in the United States, especially when such an addiction has a negative impact on students' academic performance.

Majority of the students preferred Internet over text books because it accessed the latest knowledge (Unnikrishnan, 2008). Majority of the students wanted that computer and Internet use among students should be encouraged in institutions. However, other research findings indicate that an extended presence on facebook can have harmful effects on productivity and task performance. Long hours spent on facebook decreased student's academic performance and, thus, their grades (Canales, 2009).

A study was conducted by Karpinski (2010) on the heavy Internet use and its effect on the academic achievement of adolescents. They compared the Facebook users and Non Facebook users. It was found that Facebook users Cumulative Grade Point Average (CGPA) was lower than Non-Facebook users because Facebook users spent lots of time on Facebook. Significant heavy use of Internet influenced there academic achievement.

Another study conducted by Kumar (2012) discovered that Internet use among students could stimulate their sexual attitude, behaviour and influences their premarital sex position. Further, they reported that Internet use influenced their study and academic performance as well. They also found a significant association between sexual interaction and use of Internet. Most of the boys had an unmonitored Internet service and they used it for sexual activity while no such relationship was found among girls. It was common for students to be exposed to sexual content on Internet. The study showed noteworthy relationship of having sexual interaction with academic performance and achievement specifically in boys.

Categorizing Internet users into heavy and light users Ngoumandjoka (2012) was of the view that academic work is the main reason students use the Internet on campus. Students who were classified as heavy users were found to use the Internet more for recreational purpose than the light Internet users. Thestudy further argued that more the Internet was used for academic work the more it was perceived to exert a positive influence on academic grades. A number of authors (e.g. Torres-Diaz et al., 2016) equally agreed that Internet usage had a positive impact on academic performance. They opined that students who tend to use the Internet more on educational materials were less likely to fail their examinations. In Nigeria, the impact of computer literacy on students' performance in secondary school had been explored by Aitokhuehi et al. (2014). They found that computer literate students performed better than non-computer literate students.

Leung and Lee (2012) conducted a study and reported that youth in Hong Kong who were addicted to the Internet tended to have low academic performance.Likewise, a negative correlation between Internet addiction and grades was reported among Greek high school students as well (Panayides & Walker, 2012).

Access to a home computer and Internet connection contributes to students' academic performance as well as self-learning skills (Yesilyurt et al. 2014). Taking into account access and usage of Internet by secondary school students in Nigeria, Olatokun (2008) indicated that most students believed the Internet to be far better and convenient than their school libraries. They saw it as a source for general knowledge, and hence it helped them improve their reading habits and their academic performance. The Internet is sometimes used as a supplementary learning material and has led to an improvement in students' academic performance (Siraj et al., 2015).

Vidyachathoth, Kodavanji, Kumar and Pai (2014) carried out a study and reported that excessive Internet use was evolving as a major negative consequence in adolescent and youth and they were at most risk in terms of mounting problematic Internet. The Internet addiction was associated with lowered academic performance, dullness and the lack of time for pursuing hobbies.

To make proper use of Internet in schools, college and universities, there is a need to understand the attitude of students towards Internet and the administration should know the purpose for which students were using it. A study by Pandey (2016) was carried out on attitude towards Internet and importance of Internet communication in modern education. 200 students were selected as the sample of the study and a self-developed scale was used to collect relevant data. Result showed that male students were having more positive attitude towards importance of Internet than those of female students.

However, Akende and Bamise (2017) reported that access to information can influence the academic performance of students in a positive way. The use of credible Internet resource is of greater importance for academic study, especially in high class courses which require an academic review of literature (Sahin et al., 2010). Internet use for educational purpose was found by Kim (2011) to be the heart of adolescent academic achievement. The availability of Internet was almost everywhere, most students had access to Internet on their cell phones (Ellore et al. 2014). This helped students to broaden their academic knowledge, research and assignments by accessing information worldwide and also enhances easy communication to the academic community (Siraj, et al., 2015). The use of computer and access to online resources according to Akende and Bamise (2017) are comparatively important to students.

Kumar, Kumar, Badiyani, Singh, Gupta, and Ismail (2018) conducted a study with the aim to assess the prevalence of Internet addiction among dental university students and to determineif there was any relationship of excessive Internet use with depression and academic performance among students. This was a cross sectional study which included 384 dental students from different academic years. The prevalence of Internet addiction and depression was found to be 6 per cent and 21.5 per cent, respectively. Chatting was the main purpose for Internet use. Logistic regression analysis showed that individuals who were depressed and scored less than 60 per cent marks were more likely to be addicted to Internet. The addiction to Internet had negative impact on mental health and academic performance.

Internet has become the most powerful tool in the path of education. With the advancement of Internet, the methodology of higher education has inclined towards it. Last decade has observed a complete change and notable involvement of Internet. Career shaping is now more dependent on the Internet. This revolution has changed the world of education to the extent that home classes have popped up. Today a vast amount of information is available at just a click of the mouse. Students and teachers are using a large number of learning tools. The new web technology has made it easy for students all over the world to get the skills they need to progress in society and enhance their life style. It motivates the students to acquire better thinking skills, remain well informed and grow as responsible citizens of their country. Internet has become an integral part of our lives (Jain 2016).

Based on the review of the findings of the above studies it was hypothesized that:

4(a)   **Internet Addiction will be significantly and negatively related to Academic Performance of adolescent boys.**

4(b)   **Internet Usage will be significantly and negatively related to Academic Performance of adolescent boys.**

4(c)   **Internet Addiction will be significantly and negatively related to Academic Performance of adolescent girls.**

4(d)   **Internet Usage will be significantly and negatively related to Academic Performance of adolescent girls.**

3.5 PARENT-CHILD RELATIONSHIP

There is strong evidence that the family environment has a major influence on the present and future development of children's behavior and well-being. Effective maternal authority is important in order to have a well-run family and also in maintaining parent-child relationships. Many cultural beliefs and mass media images portray parenting styles of fathers and mothers as distinct (Lamb, 1987). Proving that, studies have typically indicated that mothers are more likely to utilize an authoritative style of parenting (Smetana, 1995). These findings have been presented across different cultures, contexts and countries (Viner 2012; Lee and Yoo,2015).

3.5.1 Gender Difference and Parent-Child Relationship

A substantial amount of research aimed at explaining gender differences in young people's well-being and in unhealthy behaviors, such as adolescent offending, has looked to the family situation for explanations (Worthen 2011; Levin et al; 2012).

Dornbusch, Ritter, Liederman, Roberts and Fraleigh (1987) found that mothers were more likely to employ authoritarian style with males rather than with females. Authoritative parenting provides explanation, guidance, and communication of affect. This parenting style has a higher tendency to be associated with the child's feeling of confidence and security and positive parent-child relationship (Chen, Hastings, Rubin, Chen, Cen & Stewart, 1998).

A study was conducted by Pandey (1992) on changing pattern of parent-child relationship perception at different age levels. Objective of the study was to codify and formulate change of age and difference in perception as per gender amongst students. The sample of the study comprised 240 pupils of class VIII studying in different schools of the Tehri and Uttarkashi District. Major findings of the study were at the age of 12, the perception of father's relationship was found significant on the rejection and punishment dimensions of behavior. Boys and girls at the age of 15 perceived their fathers more dominating while girls perceived their father as more loving and affectionate with increase in age. Boys perceived their mothers more dominating and rejecting in comparison to girls. Girls and boys, at the age of 13+, perceived their mothers disciplining. At the age of 14+ no significant difference was noticed. In the case of mother –girl relationship, girls perceived mothers having more loving behavior at the age of 13+, while perception of dominating behavior increased with age, and the girls perceived their mothers as most dominating at the age of 15+. The girls felt more rejected at the age of 15+, and most protected at the age of 12+ and 13+.The girls perceived decrease in the punishing behavior of the mothers with increase in age. Disciplining behavior of the mothers was found to be highest at the age of 12 and 14 years. With increase in age there was a decreasing trend of scores on the loving dimension of parent-child relationship

Adams, Kuebli, Boyle, and Fivush (1995) found that parents' references to emotion were more frequent and varied with daughters than with sons.

The parent child interaction patterns, which involve gender specific tendencies toward emotional expression and the encouragement of emotional expression, were studied by Stewart et al., (1996). Mothers speak in softer tones and place more emphasis on thoughts and feelings with their daughters than with their sons'. Mothers also tend to model emotional expression for their daughters.Mothers reported in a study by Garner, Robertson and Smith (1997) that they express more positive emotion in the presence of their daughters than their sons. Both parents encourage their sons, more than their daughters, to control the expression of affect, to be independent, and to assume personal responsibility (Block, 1983). Garner, Robertson and Smith (1997) stated that both mothers and fathers talk more about emotions, especially positive emotion and sadness with girls than with boys.

Another study was conducted by Robinson (2000) in which he reported that parent-child dyads were similar for males and females in young adults. Parental bonding was related to parent-child relationship. Thus, when gender does make a difference in terms of parental bonding, the same difference should be seen in parent-child relationship. Besides, the analyzed data revealed that females perceived more positive affect from both parents and more father involvement compared to males. This may be due to females' tendency to develop positive interaction and better communication skills in family as they usually are more nurturing and warm compared to males (Tam & Tay, 2007).

Kajal and Kaur (2001) investigated the prevalent trend of parent-child relationship in families of middle income group. The results indicated that the boys perceived as well as expressed greater aggression and parental restrictions in comparison to girls. Boys perceived fathers as more affectionate whereas, girls perceived mothers as more affectionate.

In addition, the literature also shows that girls had stronger bonds with their parents (Svensson 2003), and that they disclosed more information to their parents about their lives (Stattin and Kerr 2000). Girls also seem to spend more time at home, which was seen as a protective factor, mainly because it limits the opportunities for offending.

Azaiza (2004) conducted a study and found that a lot of differences existed in the parent-child relations of subjects who were of Arab origin. This can be attributed to the issue of gender inequalities as well as to religious beliefs which still exist in some Eastern countries. Males were found to perceive more positive parent-child relationships compared to females. There were also major gender differences in family upbringing and parental bonding with parents being more strict and distant with their female offspring compared to males.

A study by Lloyd and Devine (2006) revealed that gender of children have affected how parents select parenting styles and the strength of the parent-child relationship. Parents tend to practice more positive parenting on females than males. In addition, females were praised and cuddled more than males; females were also being hit and shouted at less. The researchers further explained that parents tend to have better communication and were more supportive towards their daughters.

With regard to gender differences in parent-child relationships, Zhang and Fuligni ((2006) reported that females tend to establish a better relationship with their mothers and fathers as compared to their male counterparts (Rozumah & Sheereen, 2009). This is consistent with previous research that indicates females perceive a more positive quality relationship with their parents as compared to males (Tam &Yeoh, 2008).

In one of the studies it was found that adolescents perceived more psychological control from their mothers compared to their fathers. These results showed that the level of psychological control that the adolescents receive from their parents was below average and the psychological control perceived from mothers was higher than that of father (Barber, Bean, & Erickson, 2002; Rogers, Buchanan, & Winchell, 2003; Shek, 2005 and Sayil & Kindap, 2010) and males perceive more psychological control than females (Harma, 2008; Kindap, 2011; Kindap & Sayil, 2012).The analysis of the findings from the perceived behavioral control levels showed that they were above the average. The level of behavioral control that the adolescents perceived from mothers was higher than that of father. Furthermore, it was also found that females perceived higher behavioral control from both their parents compared to males. These results show that adolescents perceive behavioral control above average level from their parents, and the level of behavioral control perceived from mothers was higher than fathers. Moreover, females perceive more behavioral control compared to males. Some of the studies showed that behavioral control perceived from fathers was higher than mothers for all adolescents (Kerr & Stattin, 2000; Smetana & Daddis, 2002; Duriez, & Goossens, 2006; Aksoy, Kahraman, & Kilic, 2008; Kindap, Sayil, & Kumru, 2008 and Soenens, Vansteenkiste and Sonmez, 2011).

A study was carried out by Raj (2012) on the relationship of adolescent boys and girls from district Anantnag of Kashmir valley with their mothers and fathers. To gather information on a sample of 40 male and 40 female respondents, Parent-Child relationship Scale (Rao, 1989) was used. The results reveal that a highly significant difference was observed between the use of symbolic punishment, rejecting, loving dimension and gender of the child while no significant difference was found when protecting dimension was compared to the gender of the adolescent.

The relationship between parental authority and parent-child relationship and also to explore the differences between males and females in terms of their relationship with their parents was the major objective of Tam, Lee, Kumarasuriar and Mun (2012) study. The study was conducted on 160 participants between the ages of 17 to 25 in Malaysia. The results revealed that there was a significant parent-child relationship when the mother or father was authoritative in their parenting style. Furthermore, male participants rated both parents as significantly more authoritarian as compared to female participants. Male participants also rated both parents as significantly more permissive as compared to the ratings of their counterparts. Lastly, there was no significant difference between the genders and parent-child relationship.

In a recent study Sangma, Shantibala, Akoijam, Vizovonuo Visi and Vanlalduhsaki (2018) conducted a cross-sectional study among Class IX and X students studying in the high schools of Imphal West District of Manipur. Total sample sizes of 954 students were studied. 55 per cent students reported that they felt pressure to perform well in their academic activities and of those who felt pressure, 86.5 per cent reported that parents were mostly responsible. 39 per cent students responded that they were sleep deprived and 22.7 per cent students felt depressed due to pressure. 44.4 per cent students cope by taking pressure positively by obeying their parents/teachers and engaging in recreational activities like music, meditation, yoga etc. Pressure was more commonly felt by male students (60.3 per cent) compared to female students (51.2 per cent) and this finding was statistically significant. When students felt pressurized, 57 per cent felt that academic performance was not satisfactory as compared to 50.7 per cent students who rated their academic performance as satisfactory. The study showed that the prevalence of parental pressure is high with male students who are affected more than the females. More than one-fourth of students under pressure were feeling depressed. Nearly half of the students cope positively by obeying their parents/teachers and engaging in recreational activities like music, meditation, yoga etc.

Based on the above studies it was hypothesized that:

1(g)   Adolescent girl will score significantly higher on Protecting and Loving dimension of Parent-Child Relationship as compared to adolescent boys.

1(h)   Adolescent boys will score significantly higher on Symbolic Punishment and Symbolic Reward dimension of Parent-Child Relationship as compared to adolescent girls

3.5.2 Internet Communication and Parent Child Relationship

In a world completely dominated by technology, the time for actual face-to-face communication has reduced drastically. Most families witness both parents working to meet the demanding needs of day-to-day life. Though the development of technology has also brought in the flexible concept of working from home, the penetration of social networking into the family structure has virtually done away with need for physical interaction in the family environment.

Leung and Lee (2005) reported that among the social interaction motives, parental emotional support is found to be consistently related to Internet usage. The more emotional support from the parents an adolescent feels, the less likely they are to use the Internet. Knowing this, this makes sense that those who are more stable secure and sure with parents and/or family, will spend more time doing different activities, instead of Internet use. Again this reveals that the relationship with parents is an important issue for adolescents because interactive activities with parents promote cognitive, physical, and social development. Adolescent who lack support from parents seek social support from the experiences of interacting on the Internet (Rixhon and Shapiro, 2003; Yen and Yen, 2007).

The invention of the Internet has greatly affected 'family time'. Parents are now confronted with a new competitor for their child's time and technology has taken that space. Most parents find this new entrant creating a void in their family's closeness. In fact, parents and adolescents worry that Internet usage might have a negative effect on family communication and closeness based on family time diaries (Mesch, 2006). Families spend less time together and the cohesiveness of the family unit is diminishing as well. Traditional family dinners and other bonding experiences are becoming less common, as young individuals prefer to be online than to partake in these activities.

The main concern of a study carried out by Subrahmanyam and Greenfield (2006) was to see the effect of technology, particularly cell phones and social networking, on the family relationships. One common concern was that technology facilitated peer communication at the expense of the family. Higher levels of family conflict were associated with teens' use the Internet for social purposes, but not when they used it for education (Mesch, 2006).

Liu & Kuo (2007) identified predictors of Internet addiction. The findings showed that the quality of parent-child relationship was positively linked to the quality of respondent's interpersonal contact and frustrating interpersonal relationships raised the level of social anxiety. In addition, the results revealed that the parent–child relationship, social anxiety and interpersonal relationships all influenced Internet addiction. Lastly, those participants who experienced more social anxiety and dissatisfaction with their peer communications were more addicted to Internet.

Decline and loss of desire among adolescents for face-to-face communication with their family was related to Internet surfing has been reported byYoung (2007). The age range (14 to 18 years old) of Young's study was controlled because he brought into consideration that there may be restrictions implied in their usages of Internet by parents and also because that generation is being exposed much to technology since birth. Young reported that students in Illinois, used the Internet more often, which in turn made them to spend less time with their family. Plus, he also found that the desire for face-to-face communication with family members declined when more time was spent on the Internet. Children who spend hours on the Internet were not left with any other type of interaction or bonding time with their family (Kayany & Yelsma, 2000 and Young, 2007).

A study was conducted by Lee (2009) to find out how much time adolescents spent on computer and the amount of time they spent interacting with parents. The main aim was to investigate the use of computer for recreational and communication purposes among 1,312 adolescent from the United States (age 12 to 18) which actually replaced their time spent with their parents. Lee's result had showed an increase of 1 hour in computer-mediated communication results in a decrease of 24 minutes in time with parents. The finding showed a negative correlation among the time spent on computer and on parent-child relationship.

Psychological security and social interactive support may be the motives for adolescents with low parental support to use the Internet more than those who have high parental support. As has been pointed out by Lam (2009) that students who were very dissatisfied with their family were nearly 2.5 times more likely than those who were satisfied with their family, to be addicted to the Internet. It has also been reported by various researches that adolescents with Internet addiction consistently rated parental rearing practices as being over intrusive, punitive, and lacking in responsiveness. These findings suggested that the influences of parenting style and family function were important factors in the development of Internet dependency (Huang et. al, 2010).

Several studies have reported links between family characteristics and Internet addiction. For instance, quality of the parent–child relationship was negatively associated with the level of Internet addiction among students (Liu and Kuo, 2007). Parent–adolescent conflict (Yen, 2007) and lower satisfaction with family functioning (Ko 2007; Yen 2007) were positively related to adolescent Internet addiction.

While most research findings conclude negatively about the addition of new media to a family environment, Chen, Goh and Li (2010) welcomed the influence of new networking technologies on the parent-child relationship in Singapore. The scholars examined the intimacy level between parents and their children after the introduction of Facebook in their life. Their findings suggested that the Internet has become a new and positive mean of communication between parents and these children.

Kong and Lim (2012) reported that parent-children relationship negatively predicted cyber delinquency. Therefore, the findings have consistently shown that adolescents with low quality of parent-children relationship were more likely to become addicted to the Internet.

Research by Brigham Young University (2013) has shown that teenagers who were connected to their parents on social media felt closer to their parents in real life. Parents may not be as savvy with social media as their teenage children, but new research shows they shouldn't shy away from sending their teen a friend request on 'Facebook' or engaging them on Twitter, Instagram and other social platforms. They also found that teens, who interact with their parents on social media, had higher rates of 'prosocial' behavior. When asked about social media helping families stay connected, the reports said that social networks give an intimate look at a teenager's life. It lets parents know what their kids are going through, what their friends think is cool or fun, and helps them feel more connected to their child.

A large number of empirical studies have shown a negative association between parent-children relationship and adolescents' Internet addition. For instance, positive parent-child relationship is associated with decreased adolescents Internet addiction (Zhang et al; 2011; Denget al. 2013; Liu et al; 2013; Zhu et al. 2015), whereas, parent-children conflicts increase the risk of adolescents' Internet addiction (Yen et al; 2007; Deng, et al. 2013). Similar findings were also replicated in studies concerning electronic game addictions (Kim et al. 2007; Kwonetal, 2011). In addition, some longitudinal studies have further indicated that parent-child relationship might be a crucial antecedent of adolescents' Internet addiction.

The role that parents play in adolescents' problematic Internet use is an important influence to consider. This is the case both in regard to the environment in which problematic use may occur and in identifying potential points of intervention. Few studies have examined parental context as a correlate of problematic or addictive Internet behavior. Findings in both Asian (Chng, Li, Liau, & Khoo, 2015) and European (Siomos et al., 2012) samples of adolescents exhibiting problematic Internet use report less favorable relations with parents. Additionally, there is evidence that adolescent with less parental monitoring experience greater harassment online, such as receiving upsetting emails or instant messages and having rumors posted about them on social media (Khurana, Bleakley, Jordan, & Romer, 2014).

In a very recent study Huang, Hu, Ni, Qin and Lu (2019) aimed to explore the association between parent-child relationship and Internet addiction with the mediating effect of self-concept among Chinese adolescents. The Chinese Parent-Children Relationship Diagnostic Test, the Chinese revised edition of Tennessee Self-concept Scale, and the Chinese Internet Addiction Scale were administered to 300 junior and high school students aged 13–18 years (in grades 7–12). Results indicated that parent-children relationship was positively related to self-concept and was negatively related to Internet addiction, while self-concept was negatively related to Internet addiction among adolescents. Moreover, the association between parent-children relationship and Internet addiction was partially mediated by self-concept.

In yet another recent study Cetinkaya (2019) aimed to investigate the relationship between parental psychological and behavioral control which the adolescents perceived from their parents and Internet addiction. It employed relational survey model and was carried out with the participation of a total of 356 students (female 205, male 151) aged 14-18 years. Correlation and regression analyses were utilized to determine the level and direction of the relationship between their perceived parental psychological and behavioral control, and Internet addiction. The results yielded a positive, medium-level and meaningful relation between them. It was found that parental psychological control explained nearly 18 per cent of the total variance in Internet addiction and mothers were perceived as significantly more psychologically controlling in Internet addiction than fathers. Also, the relationship between parental behavioral control and the level of adolescents' Internet addiction was found negative and non-significant. Consequently, it was noted that perceived parental psychological control was effective in adolescents' Internet addiction tendencies, whereas behavioral control did not produce such effect.

Based on the review of the above studies it was, specifically, hypothesized that:

5(a) **Internet Addiction will be significantly and positively related to Protecting, Symbolic Punishment, Rejecting and Object Punishment dimension of Parent-Child Relationship among adolescent boys.**

5(b) **Internet Addiction will be significantly and negatively related to Loving dimension of Parent-Child Relationship among adolescent boys.**

5(c) **Internet Addiction will be significantly and positively related toProtecting, Symbolic Punishment, Rejecting and Object Punishment dimension of Parent-Child Relationship among adolescent girls.**

5(d) **Internet Addiction will be significantly and negatively related to Loving dimension of Parent-Child Relationship among adolescent girls.**

Objectives

The main objectives of the study were:

1   To measure and compare Internet Communication (Internet Addiction, Internet Usage and Internet Attitude), mental health, psychosocial adjustment, academic performance and parent-child relationship among adolescent boys and girls.

2   To assess and compare the effect of Internet Communication(Internet Addiction, Internet Usage and Internet Attitude) on Mental Health of adolescents boys and girls.

3   To evaluate and compare the effect of Internet Communication (Internet Addiction, Internet Usage and Internet Attitude) on Psychosocial Adjustment of adolescents boys and girls.

4   To measure and compare the outcome of Internet Communication (Internet Addiction, Internet Usage and Internet Attitude) on Academic Performance of adolescent boys and girls.

5   To asses and compare the impact of Internet Communication (Internet Addiction, Internet Usage and Internet Attitude) on Parent-Child Relationship among adolescents boys and girls.

Hypotheses

The hypotheses tested in the study were developed and presented in the earlier sections of this chapter. The specific hypotheses tested in the present investigation are summarized in this section for ready reference of the reader. Specifically:

1(a)   Adolescent boys will score significantly higher in terms of Internet Addiction, Internet Usage and Internet Attitude as compared to adolescent girls.

1(b)   Adolescent girls will score significantly higher in terms of Depression, General Positive Affect, Emotional Ties and Life Satisfaction as compared to adolescent boys.

1(c)   Adolescent boys will score significantly higher in terms of Anxiety and Loss of Behavioural/Emotional Control as compared to adolescent girls.

1(d)   Adolescent boy will score significantly higher in terms of Emotional and School Adjustment as compared to adolescent girls.

1(e)   Adolescent girls will score significantly higher in terms of Family, Health and Social Adjustment as compared to adolescent boys.

1(f)   Adolescent girls will score significantly higher in terms of Academic Performance as compared to adolescent boys.

1(g)   Adolescent girls will score significantly higher on Protecting and Loving dimension of Parent-Child Relationship as compared to adolescent boys.

1(h)   Adolescent boys will score significantly higher on Symbolic punishment and Symbolic Reward dimension of Parent-Child Relationship as compared to adolescent girls.

1.   Internet Communication (Internet Addiction, Internet Usage and Internet Attitude) have a differential impact on the mental health of adolescent boys and girls. The specific hypotheses that were formulated are:

2(a)   Internet Addiction will be significantly and positively related to Anxiety, Depression, Loss of Behavioral /Emotional Control among adolescent boys.

2(b)   Internet Addiction will be significantly and negatively related to General Positive Affect, Emotional Ties and Life Satisfaction among adolescent boys.

2(c)   Internet Addiction will be significantly and positively related to Anxiety, Depression, and Loss of Behavioral /Emotional Control among adolescent girls.

2(d)   Internet Addiction will be significantly and negatively related to General Positive Affect, Emotional Ties and Life Satisfaction among adolescent girls.

2(e)   Internet Usage will be significantly and positively related to Anxiety and Depression among adolescent boys.

2(f)   Internet Usage will be significantly and positively related to Anxiety and Depression among adolescent girls

2(e)   Internet Addiction will be significantly and negatively related to general positive affect, emotional ties and life satisfaction among adolescent boys

2(f)   Internet Addiction will be significantly and negatively related to general positive affect, emotional ties and life satisfaction among adolescent girls

3. Internet Communication (Internet Addiction, Internet Usage and Internet Attitude) can lead to certain psychosocial adjustment problems among adolescent boys and girls. The specific hypotheses that were formulated are:

3(a)   Internet Addiction will be significantly and positively related to Emotional, Family, Health, Social and School Adjustment of adolescent boys.

3(b)   Internet Addiction will be significantly and positively related to Emotional, Family, Health, Social and School adjustment of adolescent girls.

4. Internet Communication (Internet Addiction, Internet Usage and Internet Attitude) will affect the academic performance of adolescent boys and girls. The specific hypotheses that were formulated are:

4(a)   Internet Addiction will be significantly and negatively related to Academic Performance of adolescent boys.

4(b)   Internet Usage will be significantly and negatively related to Academic Performance of adolescent boys.

4(c)   Internet Addiction will be significantly and negatively related to Academic Performance of adolescent girls.

4(d)   Internet Usage will be significantly and positively related to Internet Usage will be significantly and negatively related to Academic Performance of adolescent girls.

5. Internet Communication (Internet Addiction, Internet Usage and Internet Attitude) will also be affecting the parent-child relationship of adolescent boys and girls. The specific hypotheses that were formulated are:

5(a)   Internet Addiction will be significantly and positively related to Protecting, Symbolic Punishment, Rejecting and Object Punishment dimension of Parent-Child Relationship among adolescent boys.

5(b)   Internet Addiction will be significantly and negatively related to Loving dimension of Parent-Child Relationship among adolescent boys.

5(c)   Internet Addiction will be significantly and positively related toProtecting, Symbolic Punishment, Rejecting and Object Punishment dimension of Parent-Child Relationship among adolescent girls.

5(d)   Internet Addiction will be significantly and negatively related to Loving dimension of Parent-Child Relationship among adolescent girls.

CHAPTER-4
METHODOLOGY

The systematic and scientific research is reflected in its methodology. Methodology is usually a guideline system for solving a problem, with specific components such as phases, tasks, methods, techniques and tools. When people talk of research methodology they do not only talk of the research methods but also consider the logic behind the methods they used in the context of research study and explain why a particular method or technique was used or not used so that research results are capable of being evaluated either by the researcher himself or by others. Thus, it indicates the practical way in which the whole research project has been organized, planned and executed.

The aim of the present research work was to assess adolescent use of the Internet Communication and Socially Interactive Technologies (SITs) and its effect on Mental Health, Psychosocial Adjustment, Academic Performance and Parent-Child Relationship and to investigate how gender moderates those relationships.

4.1 THE SETTING

Total population of Uttar Pradesh as per the Census figures of 2011 was 199,812,341, of which male and female were 104,480,510 and 95,331,831, respectively. The population of Uttar Pradesh forms 16.50 per cent the total population of India in 2011. The sex ratio in the year 2011 was 928 females for every 1000 male and that was quite low as compared to the national average. Literacy rate in Uttar Pradesh has seen upward trend and is 67.68 per cent as per 2011 Census figures. Out of that, male literacy stands at 77.28 per cent while female literacy is at 57.18 per cent. Uttar Pradesh holds the first position in terms of population and is the most populated state of the country. The state contributes around 17 per cent of the number of people in the country. The population density is about 828 persons per square kilometer and it surely makes it one of the densely populated states of India.

Lucknow is the capital city of the Indian state of Uttar Pradesh and is also the administrative headquarters of the eponymous District and Division. It is the eleventh most populous city and the twelfth most populous urban agglomeration of India. Lucknow has always been known as a multicultural city that flourished as a North Indian cultural and artistic hub, and the seat of power of Nawabs in the 18th and 19th centuries. It continues to be an important centre of governance, administration, education, commerce, aerospace, finance, pharmaceuticals, technology, design, culture, tourism, music and poetry.

Lucknow district of Uttar Pradesh has total population of 4,589,838 as per the Census, 2011. Out of which 2,394,476 are males while 2,195,362 are females. Population density of the city is 2286 persons per km^2. As per State Census 2011 out of total population, 66.2 per cent people live in urban areas while 33.8 per cent live in the rural areas. Literacy rate of Lucknow city is 85.88 per cent higher than state average of 67.68 per cent. In Lucknow, Male literacy is around 89.95 per cent while female literacy rate is 80.11 per cent which is considered very descent compared to last census of 2011. A large proportion of population in the city is educated.

The Lucknow Cantonment Board is the only cantonment board located in and around the city of Lucknow. Total geographical area of the cantonment is around 28 square kilometer. It has a population of 63,003 of which 36,586 are males while 26,417 are females as per report released by Census of India 2011. In Lucknow Cantonment Board, female sex ratio is 928 against state average of 912.

Army Public Schools (APS) is a system of public schools established for imparting education to the children of the Indian armed forces personnel. With over 130 schools throughout the country, it is one of the largest chains of schools in India. It is controlled by the Army Welfare Education Society (AWES), which was established in 1983, has over the years established more than 135 Army public schools and 249 Army pre-primary schools across India, and also several institutions of higher education. The schools are generally managed by the armyregional commands following the CBSE pattern of education. Admission is granted on a priority basis to wards of Army personnel. All Army schools have a chairman who is a senior Indian Army officer of Brigadier rank and a patron who is of Major General Rank. The criteria of getting admission in Army Public Schools are 90 per cent for defence children and 10 per cent civilians.

4.2 SAMPLE

A purposive sampling approach was employed to select a total sample of 513 students. The data was collected from the three Army Public Schools located at Lucknow Cantt. The data from students was taken after obtaining permission from the school Principals to conduct the study in their respective schools.In the present study, only 2 per cent children were civilians and 98 per cent children were from army background. Participants, in the study were 9th and 11th grade students in the age range of 14 to 18 years. All the students of 9th and 11th grade were administered the protocol. The class strength comprised of on an average of 40 students per class. The test was administered to the students in two settings. Three sections each of 9th and 11th standard from each of the three selected schools were taken. Initially, total number of 720 students participated in the study but due to incomplete responses, incorrect responses and in certain cases non-availability of the students in the second day of test finally only those students were retained for the final data analysis who were present on both the days of test execution, completed the test as per the instructions and had access to Internet at home. The final sample, thus, comprised of 513 students. Out of which there were 260 boys and 253 girls. Out of the final total sample of 513 adolescents 280 and 233 were from 9th and 11th standard, respectively. The test was administered to the students during their regular school time in their respective classes in the presence of their teacher and researcher.

4.3 BACKGROUND CHARACTERISTICS OF THE ADOLESCENTS

The demographic details of the adolescents are presented in Table 4.1As it is evident from Table 4.1, the adolescents who participated in the study were in the age group of 14 years (23.39 per cent), 15 years (28.85 per cent), 16 years (4.34 per cent), 17 years (23.98 per cent) and 18 years (18.91 per cent), respectively. Overwhelming 97.07 per cent adolescents belonged to defense families of India and 97.66 per cent mothers were homemakers.

Approximately 9 per cent of adolescents belonged to families with household monthly income of above Rs 1 Lac whereas the majority, i.e., an overwhelming majority of 83.43 per cent lied between Rs 50,000 to Rs 70,000 and only 8 per cent lied in the Rs 30,000 to Rs 40,000 bracket. This indicates that most of the participants belonged to middle class families, with decent standard of living.

Table 4.1: Demographic characteristics of the Adolescent

Sr. No.	Background Characteristics	Number	Percentage
1.	**Gender**		
	Male	260	50.68
	Female	253	49.32
2.	**Class**		
	9th	280	54.58
	11th	233	45.42
3.	**Age**		
	14	120	23.39
	15	148	28.85
	16	25	4.87
	17	123	23.98
	18	97	18.91
4.	**Father's Occupation**		
	Defense Background	498	97.07
	Civil Background	15	2.93
5.	**Mother's Occupation**		
	Home Makers	501	97.66
	Employed	12	2.34
6.	**Income**		
	1 lac and above	45	9
	50000-70000	428	83.44
	30000-40000	40	7

4.4 TOOLS USED

Some standardized scales and questionnaire have been used to collect data in the present research study. In order to measure the adolescent's use of Internet and Socially Interactive Technologies (SITs) Internet Addiction Test of Kimberly Young (1996) and detailed questionnaire regarding the Internet Usage and Internet Attitude was used. For measuring the

Mental Health of selected sample Mental Health Inventory (MHI-38) was administered. Global Adjustment Scale (GAS- Form S) was used to evaluate the Psychosocial Adjustment. Parent-Child Relationship scale (Rao, 1989) was administered to assess the Parent-Child Relationship of the selected students. Academic performance of adolescents has been evaluated on the basis of their academic grades in the final examination of previous class attended.

4.4.1Internet Communication

4.4.1a Internet Addiction Test

Internet Addiction Test (IAT) developed by Kimberly Young (1996) is a reliable and valid measure of addictive use of Internet. This test was used to measure the addiction of the Internet among adolescent. It is a 20-item scale covering the degree to which use of Internet disrupts everyday life (work, sleep, relationships, etc.). Each item has been scored on a 5 point likert scale. The score ranges from 20 to 100. On the basis of the total score obtained on the test, the individual is placed into one of three categories: average online user (from 20 to 39) moderate Internet use (from 40 to 69); and excessive Internet use (from 70 to 100).The higher the score, the greater the level of addiction. The internal reliability of the scale is 0.93.

4.4.1bInternet Usage and Internet Attitude Questionnaire

In order to measure the Internet Usage and Internet Attitude of the adolescents, a questionnaire has been developed. Questions about Internet Usage and Internet Attitude regarding Socially Interactive Technologies (SITs) use has been taken from Windham (2008). Only those items have been selected from the tests which were applicable as per the Indian settings. This questionnaire included the items to assess the student's Internet and SITs (Socially Interactive Technologies) usage as well as their attitudes towards Internet.

Internet Usage

Items are designed to explore the Internet Usage of boys and girls to measure the usage of Internet components. It is an 18 items questionnaire covering the items related to the usage of SIT's (Socially interactive Technologies). Each item has been scored on a 5 point likert scale. The score range is from 18 to 90.On the basis of the total score obtained on the questionnaire, the individual is placed into the average category ofuser (from 18 to 40);moderate user (from 41 to

63); and excessive user (from 64 to 90) of Internet. Higher the score higher is the usage of the Internet among adolescents.

Internet Attitude

This questionnaire of Internet Attitude is designed to explore the value, beliefs and feelings of individuals regarding Internet.It is a 12 items questionnaire which covers the items related to the attitude of individual towards the Internet. Each item has been scored on a 5 point likert scale. The score ranges from 12 to 60.On the basis of the total score obtained on the test, average attitude towards Internet (from 12 to 25) moderate attitude scores (from 26 to 39); and has problematic attitude (from 40 to 60). Higher scores indicate the significant problematic attitude of individuals towards Internet.

4.4.2Mental Health

Mental Health Inventory (MHI-38)

The Mental Health Inventory (MHI-38) was designed by Davies, Sherbourne, Peterson and Ware in 1998. It is a 38 item measure designed to assess the multi dimension nature ofpsychological distress and psychological well-being, including: Anxiety, Depression, Loss of Behavioural/Emotional Control, General Positive Affect, Emotional Ties and Life Satisfaction (Davies, Sherbourbe, Peterson and Ware, 1998). The Mental Health Inventory has a reported .93 cronbach alpha rating whereas its abbreviated version has .82.

MHI-38 Subscales and Scoring

All of the 38 MHI-38 items, except two, are scored on a six-point scale (range 1-6). Items 9 and 28 are the exception, each scored on a five-point scale (range 1-5). The MHI-38 has been categorized into six subscales namely Anxiety, Depression, Loss of Behavioral / Emotional Control, General Positive Affect, Emotional Ties and Life Satisfaction, which are further divided into two global scales i.e. psychological distress and psychological well- being.

Scoring the subscales

The subscales are scored in two steps: (1) item scoring; and (2) the subscale scoring. Of the 38 items, 35 are used to score the six mental health subscales. Each item appears in only one subscale. Table 4.2 shows the mapping of items to the various subscales. Three items (2, 22 and

38) are not used to score the subscales but they are incorporated for scoring two global scales (Psychological Distress and Psychological Well-Being).

Table 4.2: Item composition of the six MHI subscales included in MHI-38

Subscales	Component items	Subscale directionality	Subscale raw score range
Anxiety	Items 3, 11, 13, 15, 25, 29, 32, 33 and 35	Higher scores = greater Anxiety	9-54
Depression	Items 9, 19, 30 and 36	Higher scores = greater Depression	4-23
Loss of Behavioral/Emotional Control	Items 8, 14, 16, 18, 20, 21, 24, 27 and 28	Higher scores = greater Loss of Behavioral / Emotional Control	9-53
General Positive Affect	Items 4, 5, 6, 7, 12, 17, 26, 31, 34 and 37	Higher scores = greater Positive Affect	10-60
Emotional Ties	Items 10 and 23	Higher scores = stronger Emotional Ties	2-12
Life Satisfaction	1	Higher score=greater life satisfaction	1-6

Note:Three items (2, 22, and 38) are not used to score the subscales.

After scoring items as indicated, items belonging to each subscale are summed to give subscale scores.

Table 4.3:Coding rule for MHI-38 Items used to score subscales

Item No.	Code value	Recorded value
1,3,4,5,6,7,10,11,12,13,15,16,17,19,20,21,23,24,25,26,27, 29,30,31,32,33,34,35,36,37	1	6
	2	5
	3	4
	4	3
	5	2
	6	1
8,14,18	1	1
	2	2
	3	3
	4	4
	5	5
	6	6

9,28	1	5
	2	4
	3	3
	4	2
	5	1

4.4.3 Psychosocial Adjustment

Global Adjustment Scale

In order to measure the Psychosocial adjustment of adolescents the Global Adjustment Scale (GAS Form S) developed and designed by Psy-com services (1994) has been used in the present study. The GAS Form S has 120 items, which covers five adjustment areas namely emotional, family, health, school and social. The test items have been selected from a total pool of more than 400 items that had been tested and refined in programmatic studies on adaptive behavior. This test has been standardized on more than 800 protocols tested at more than 7 locations throughout the country.

Reliability

The reliability of the test was calculated as split half reliability and test retest reliability coefficient with one month interval, the reliability was computed for over 300 students using Spearman-Brown formula. The scale was divided into two parts using odd-even method. The test-retest reliability was also calculated for the present scale by calculating the correlation of coefficient between two sets of scores of the same student on the same scale with one month time interval.

Table 4.4: Test Retest and Split Half test Reliability coefficient of the five subscales

Dimension	Test-retest(one month interval)	Split half
Emotional	.74	.79
Family	.65	.69
Health	.69	.79

Social	.75	.83
School	.72	.78

Validity: The factor analysis verified the existence and structure of the five adjustment areas.

Table 4.5:Factorial validity coefficients of GAS Form S for five subscales

Dimensions	Validity coefficients
Emotional	.72
Family	.61
Health	.69
Social	.69
School	.71

Scoring

The scoring procedure in GAS Form S is quiet objective and simple. Transparent stencil scoring keys are available and to be used for this purpose. Each answer was scored either as 2 or 1 as indicated by the numbers printed above the circles. These scores are then added for each adjustment area and written at the bottom of the answer sheet in the space provided for that area. A high score on emotional adjustment is symptomatic of more general unresolved problems of learning to accept, express and control one's emotions. A high score on family adjustment tends to be associated with conflicts and persistent tensions in the family. High scores on health adjustment reflects a history of poor health and an excessive preoccupation with one's body mentally or both. The students who score high on social adjustment react with complicated and often paradoxical responses and they tend to be highly dissatisfied with school conditions. High scores on social adjustment indicate respondents' hostile nature. Thus, high scores on all the sub domains of Psychosocial adjustment have to be interpreted as low adjustment. Such people are usually very confident and are not satisfied with what others think about them. Steps for scoring are as follows:

1) Before starting the scoring procedure, examiner should ensure that the subject has answered all the questions on the answer sheet.

2) If more than 15 questions are skipped, the test is considered invalid and should not be scored.

This is a self-administered test containing120 items to measure adjustment of the subject in five areas namely family, health, social, emotions and school. But items on "Sex Adjustment" were not included for the research for their inappropriateness for adolescents.Each item in the test measures these adjustment areas as indicated below:

Emotional: 1,7,13,19,25,31,37,43,49,55,61,67,73,79,85,91,97,103,109,115

Family: 2,8,14,20,26,32,38,44,50,56,62,68,74,80,86,92,98,104,110,116

Health:3,9,15,21,27,33,39,45,51,57,63,69,75,81,87,93,99,105,111,117

Social: 4,10,16,22,28,34,40,46,52,58,64,70,76,82,88,94,100,106,112,118

School: 6,12,18,24,30,36,42,48,54,60,66,72,78,84,90,96,102,108,114,120

Raw scores were converted to Sten scores by the following procedure Sten 1-2=Excellent, Sten 3-4=Good, Sten 5-6=Average, Sten 7-8=Unsatisfactory, Sten 9-10 = Poor.Thus, high scores have to be interpreted as low adjustment.

4.4.4Academic Performance

Academic performance of the selected sample has been evaluated on the basis of the total academic grades secured in the final examination of the previous class attended The average of grade points obtained in five basic subject areas: Math, Science, English, Hindi and Social Studies. The grade scores for final data analysis for each student were obtained from the records of the school and were converted in to percentages.

4.4.5Parent Child Relationship

Parent -Child Relationship Scale

Parent-child relationship scale has been developed by Nalini Rao (1989) and it measures characteristic behavior of parents as experienced by their children. The theoretical importance of the child's perception of parent's behavior for understanding socio-psychological personal development has been emphasized by a number of social scientists. Their main focus is on the issue that it is the subject that interprets the interaction between him and his parents who is pertinent and for him, it is his own definition of the situation that is significant. It is also observed that the parental behavior affects the child's ego development only to the extent in the form in which he perceives it.

The data available on the items of the scale has been grouped into fairly universal dimensions of children's experience of family interaction with the two parent factor. This tool contains 100 items categorized into ten dimensions namely: Protecting, Symbolic Punishment, Rejection, Object Punishment, Demanding, Indifferent, Symbolic Reward, Loving, Object Reward and Neglecting. Items of the scale are arranged in the same order as dimensions and they rotate in a cycle through the scale. Each respondent scores the tool for both father and mother separately. Items are common for both the parents except for three items which are different, in father and mother forms due to the nature of variation in the parental and maternal relationship with children.

In the present study the scale was scored only for the mothers. The perceptions and experience of adolescents regarding their mothers' interaction with them was taken into consideration. The scores of boys and girls perception on the characteristic behavior of mothers as experienced by them were recorded as measure of Parent Child Relationship.

Respondent has beenasked to rate statements as per their own perception of their relationship with themother on a five point scale, ranging from 'Always' to 'Very Rarely' weighted 5,4,3,2, and 1, respectively, on the scale. Every respondent obtain 10 for mother form on the ten dimensions of the scale. Each subscale yields a score by summing the ratings of the respondent on each item of ten subscales. High score indicates a person's perception of more of that respective dimension from mother and father.

4.5STATISITCAL ANALYSIS

For analyzing the data the following statistical techniques have been used:

4.5.1 Mean, Standard Deviation and t-test

t-test has been administered to find out the significance of difference between the mean scores of boys and girls on Internet Communication (Internet Addiction, Internet Usage and Internet Attitude) six dimensions of Mental Health(namely anxiety, depression, loss of behavioral / emotional control, general positive affect, emotional ties and life satisfaction), five dimensions of Psychosocial Adjustment (namely emotional, family, health, social and school), Academic Performance and 10 dimensions of Parent-Child Relationship (namely protecting, symbolic punishment, rejecting, object punishment, demanding, indifferent, symbolic reward, loving, object reward and neglecting).

4.5.2 Correlation Analysis

Pearson Product Moment correlation has beencomputed separately forboys and girls to see therelationship among the Internet Communication (Internet Addiction, Internet Usage and Internet Attitude) six dimensions of Mental Health(namely anxiety, depression, loss of behavioral / emotional control, general positive affect, emotional ties and life satisfaction), five dimensions of Psychosocial Adjustment (namely emotional, family, health, social and school), Academic Performance and 10 dimensions of Parent-Child Relationship (namely protecting, symbolic punishment, rejecting, object punishment, demanding, indifferent, symbolic reward, loving, object reward and neglecting).

4.5.3 Regression Analysis

Step wise Regression analysis has been carried out to assess the significant predictors of the dependent variables namely six dimensions of Mental Health (namely anxiety, depression, loss of behavioral / emotional control, general positive affect, emotional ties and life satisfaction), five dimensions of Psychosocial Adjustment (namely emotional, family, health, social and school),and Academic Performance. The predictor variables were Internet Communication (Internet Addiction,Internet Usage and Internet Attitude) and ten dimensions of Parent-Child Relationship (namely protecting, symbolic punishment, rejecting, object punishment, demanding, indifferent, symbolic reward, loving, object reward and neglecting). The stepwise regression analysis has been carried out separately for boys and girls.

CHAPTER-5
RESULTS

The aim of the present investigation was to measure the Internet Communication (Internet Addiction, Internet Usage and Internet Attitude) and its impact on the Mental Health, Psychosocial Adjustment, Academic Performance and Parent-Child Relationship among adolescent boys and girls in the state of Uttar Pradesh. The sample consisted of 513 students (Boys=260, Girls= 253) studying in 9th and 11th standard.The results of the study are presented in the following order:

Preliminary Results

t- test was computed in order to find out the significance of difference between the mean scores obtained by adolescent boys and adolescent girls on Internet Communication (Internet Addiction, Internet Usage and Internet Attitude), six variables of Mental health (namely anxiety, depression, loss of behavioral/ emotional control, general positive affect, emotional ties and life satisfaction), five variables of Psychosocial Adjustment (namely emotional, family, health, social, & school),Academic Performance andten variables of Parent-Child Relationship (namely protecting, symbolic punishment, rejecting, object punishment, demanding, indifferent, symbolic reward, loving, object reward and neglecting).

Correlation Analysis

Pearson's Product Moment Correlation was applied to find out the correlation between the Internet Communication (Internet Addiction, Internet Usage andInternet Attitude), six variables of Mental Health (namely anxiety, depression, loss of behavioral/ emotional control, general positive affect, emotional ties and life satisfaction), five variables of Psychosocial Adjustment (namely emotional, family, health, social& school),Academic Performance andten variables of Parent-Child Relationship (namely protecting, symbolic punishment, rejecting, object punishment, demanding, indifferent, symbolic reward, loving, object reward and neglecting) among adolescent boys and girls. The results of correlation are presented in the following order:

1. Correlation of Internet Communication (Internet Addiction, Internet Usage and Internet Attitude), Mental Health, Psychosocial Adjustment, Academic Performance and Parent-Child Relationship among adolescent boys.

2. Correlation ofInternet Communication (Internet Addiction, internet Usage and Internet Attitude), Mental Health, Psychosocial Adjustment, Academic Performance and Parent-Child Relationship among adolescent girls.

Stepwise Regression Analysis

Stepwise regression analysis was carried out in order to find out the most significant predictors of six variables of Mental health (namely anxiety, depression, loss of behavioral/ emotional control, general positive affect, emotional ties and life satisfaction), five variables of Psychosocial Adjustment (namely emotional, family, health, social,& school) and Academic Performance. The predicted variables were Internet Communication (Internet Addiction, Internet Usage and Internet Attitude) and ten dimensions of Parent-Child Relationship (namely protecting, symbolic punishment, rejecting, object punishment, demanding, indifferent, symbolic reward, loving, object reward and neglecting).The regression analysis were computed separately for boys and girls. The results of regression analysis are presented in the following order:

1. Stepwise regression analysis for adolescent boys

2. Stepwise regression analysis for adolescent girls.

5.1 PRELIMINARY RESULTS

t- test was carried out to find out the significance of difference between the mean scores of adolescent boys and adolescent girls on Internet Communication (Internet Addiction, Internet Usage and Internet Attitude), six variables of Mental Health (namely anxiety, depression, loss of behavioral/ emotional control, general positive affect, emotional ties and life satisfaction), five variables of Psychosocial Adjustment (namely emotional, family, health, social& school),Academic Performance andten variables of Parent-Child Relationship (namely protecting, symbolic punishment, rejecting, object punishment, demanding, indifferent, symbolic reward, loving, object reward and neglecting).The results of t -test are presented in Table 5.1 and graphically depicted in Figure 5.1.

5.1.1Internet Communication

Internet Addiction Test (IAT) developed by Kimberly Young (1996) was used to measure the addiction of the Internet among adolescent. The 20-item scale covering the degree to which use of internet disrupts everyday life (work, sleep, relationships, etc.). Each item has been scored on a 5 point likert scale. In order to measure the Internet Usage and Internet Attitude of the adolescents, a questionnaire has been developed. Questions about Internet Usage and Internet Attitude regarding Socially Interactive Technologies (SITs) use has been taken from Windham (2008). Only those items have been selected from the tests which were applicable as per the Indian settings. This questionnaire included the items to assess the student's Internet and SITs (Socially Interactive Technologies) usage as well as their attitudes towards internet.

The present section shows the comparative results of Internet Communication which covers the Internet Addiction, Internet Usage and Internet Attitude among adolescent boys and girls.

5.1.1a Internet Addiction

It is depicted in Table 5.1 that adolescent boys (M = 65.94) have significantly (t = 6.830, p <.05) scored higher on Internet Addiction as compared to adolescent girls (M= 52.63).This indicates that boys are more addicted to internet as compared to girls.

5.1.1bInternet Usage

Furthermore, the results reveal that boys (M= 61.00) have significantly (t = 2.90, p <.05) scored higher on Internet Usage as compared to girls (M = 56.36), as is shown inTable 5.1.This indicates that boys indulge in higher usage of internet services as compared to their female counterparts.

5.1.1cInternet Attitude

The calculated t- value (t = 5.91, p<.05) shown in the perusal of Table 5.1 clearly depicts that adolescent boys (M= 44.31) have significantly scored higher on Internet Attitude as compared to female students (M = 38.08).The results indicate that the boys beliefs, values and feelings are more inclined towards internet as compared to girls.

Thus, the above mentioned results substantiate the hypothesis **1(a)** that **"Adolescent boys will score significantly higher in terms of Internet Addiction, Internet Usage and Internet Attitude as compared to adolescent girls".**

It can be concluded from the above mentioned results that adolescent boys have significantly outscored on all the dimensions of Internet Communication namely internet addiction, internet usage and internet attitude than their female counterparts.

5.1.2 Mental Health

The mental health of boys and girls was measured by administering Mental Health Inventory (MHI-38) designed by Davies, Sherbourne, Peterson and Ware (1998) among the selected sample of adolescents. The inventory has six sub domains, namely anxiety, depression, loss of behavioral/emotional control, general positive affect, emotional ties and life satisfaction. t-test was carried out to see the significance of difference between the means of the two groups.

The results of Mental Health among adolescent boys and girls are presented in Table 5.1 and graphically depicted in Figure 5.1.

5.1.2aAnxiety

Table 5.1 shows that adolescent boys (M = 31.30) scored higher on the mean score on Anxiety as compared to adolescent girls (M= 30.73) but the difference could not reach the level of significance (t =.534, n.s.).

5.1.2bDepression

Furthermore, it is clear from the results that adolescent girls (M =15.64) significantly (t = 2.01, p <.05) scored higher on Depression as compared to adolescent boys (M=14.62) as is presented in Table 5.1, indicating that the girls are experiencing higher level of depression as compared to boys.

Table 5.1: Showing the Mean, Standard Deviation and t-ratio of adolescent boys and adolescent girls on the Internet communication (Internet Addiction, Internet Usage and Internet Attitude), Mental Health, Psychosocial Adjustment, Academic Performance and Parent Child Relationship

Sr.No.	Variables	Adolescent Boys (N=260)		Adolescent Girls (N=253)		t-ratio
		M	SD	M	SD	
A	IAT	65.948	22.2992	52.632	21.2826	**6.830****
B	**Internet Usage**	61.004	18.6154	56.364	17.1312	**2.900****
C	**Internet Attitude**	44.312	10.9742	38.084	12.5246	**5.914****
D	**Mental Health**					
1	Anxiety	31.300	14.4579	30.736	8.3340	.534
2	Depression	14.620	6.6178	15.644	4.5888	**2.011****
3	Loss of Behavioral/Emotional Control	32.696	10.7507	30.308	9.8477	**2.590****
4	General positive affect	32.692	7.9495	36.624	10.9461	**4.596****
5	Emotional Ties	6.308	2.1873	6.844	2.0149	**2.850***
6	Life Satisfaction	3.452	1.3292	4.256	1.3965	**6.594****
E	**Psycho social Adjustment**					
1	Emotional	5.520	1.6627	6.212	2.0882	**4.099****
2	family	4.224	1.6200	4.376	1.5506	1.072
3	Health	5.372	1.5398	4.828	1.4390	**4.081****
4	Social	4.616	2.2398	4.668	1.8163	.285
5	Sex	4.212	1.5180	4.320	1.5554	.786
6	School	4.224	1.5043	4.612	1.7463	**2.662 ****
F	**Academic Performance**	72.768	12.9544	78.032	12.6446	**4.598****
G	**Parent Child Relationship**					
1	Protecting	2.656	1.1344	3.608	.9727	**10.073****
2	Symbolic Punishment	3.644	.9721	2.368	.8693	**15.471****
3	Rejection	3.404	1.0378	3.304	1.0469	1.073
4	Object Punishment	3.332	1.0129	3.320	1.1379	.125
5	Demanding	3.260	1.0606	3.256	1.1849	.040
6	Indifferent	3.440	1.0052	3.476	1.0535	.391
7	Symbolic Reward	3.364	1.0216	3.340	1.0682	.257
8	Loving	3.372	1.0536	3.380	1.0956	.083
9	Object Reward	3.348	1.0879	3.440	1.0289	.971
10	Neglecting	3.384	1.0319	3.448	1.0789	.678

**p<.01 and *p<.05

Figure 5.1: **Showing the Mean difference among adolescent boys and girls on the Internet communication (Internet Addiction, Internet Usage and Internet Attitude), Mental Health, Psychosocial Adjustment, Academic Performance and Parent Child Relationship**

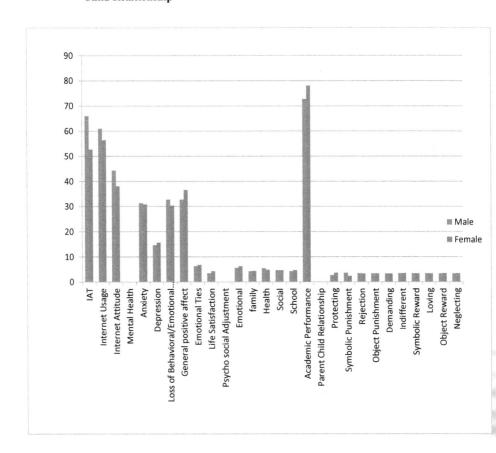

5.1.2c Loss of behavioral/Emotional Control

The mean and t- values (t = 2.59, p<.05)as shown in Table 5.1 reveals that adolescent boys (M =32.69) scored significantlyhigher on Loss of Behavioral/Emotional Control as compared to adolescent girls (M= 30.30) which clearly shows that girls are better regulated in terms of their emotional and behavioral control as compared to boys.

5.1.2dGeneral Positive Affect

The mean score of adolescent girls (M = 36.62) is significantly (t = 4.5, p<.05) higher on General Positive Affect as compared to boys (M= 32.69) as is shown in Table 5.1. It depicts that girls in the present investigation have a more positive general affect as compared to boys.

5.1.2eEmotional Ties

Likewise, the results presented in Table 5.1 reveal that adolescent girls (M =6.84) significantly (t = 2.85, p<.05) scored higher on the dimension of Emotional Ties as compared to adolescent boys (M= 6.30).These results reflect that girls in the present study have better emotional ties, interpersonal relationships and emotional attachments as compared to male adolescents.

5.1.2f Life satisfaction

Table 5.1 also signifies the significant difference on the dimension of Life Satisfaction among adolescent boys and girls. The girls (M = 4.25) have significantly (t = 6.59, p <.05) higher life satisfaction as compared to adolescent boys (M= 3.45).The results indicate that girls are more contended, satisfied and happy as compared to the boys.

Therefore, the hypothesis **1(b) "Adolescent girls will score significantly higher in terms of Depression, General Positive Affect, Emotional Ties and Life Satisfaction as compared to adolescent boys"** stands proved and hypotheses **1(c)** that **"Adolescent boys will score significantly higher in terms of Anxiety and Loss of Behavioral/Emotional control as compared to adolescent girls"** is partially proved.

From the above mentioned results it can be concluded that on the six dimensions ofMental Health girls have significantly outscored boys on the dimension of depression, general positive affect, emotional ties and life satisfaction, whereas boys significantly outscored girls on the dimension of Loss of Behavioral/emotional control. Results indicate that girls are significantly better on the psychological wellbeing except depression. Boys have significantly higher psychological distress in terms of loss of behavioral/emotional control.

5.1.3 Psychosocial Adjustment

To measure the psychosocial adjustment of adolescents the Global Adjustment Scale (GAS Form S) developed and designed by Psy-com services (1994) has been used in the present study. The GAS Form S has 100 items, which covers five adjustment areas namely emotional, family, health, school and social.

The results of Psychosocial Adjustment among adolescent boys and girls is presented in Table 5.1 and graphically depicted in Figure 5.1.Out of the five variables of Psychosocial Adjustment only three variables (namely emotional, health and school adjustment) emerged to have significant differences between male and female students. **As per the scoring instructions of the scale high scores have to be interpreted as poor adjustment.**

5.1.3a Emotional Adjustment

The mean score of adolescent girls (M = 6.21) is significantly (t = 4.098, p <.05) high on emotional adjustment as compared to adolescent boys (M= 5.52) as is presented in Table 5.1.Higher scores show poor emotional adjustment. Thus, the results shows that boys are better regulated in terms of their emotions as compared to girls.

5.1.3b Family Adjustment

Table 5.1 shows that adolescent girls (M = 4.37) scored higher on the mean score on family adjustment as compared to adolescent boys (M= 4.22) but the difference could not reach the level of significance (t =1.07, n.s.).

5.1.3c Health Adjustment

A perusal of Table 5.1 further reveals that adolescent boys (M=5.37) significantly (t = 4.08, p = <.05) scored higher on health adjustment as compared to girls (M = 4.82). The result depicts that girls are better adjusted in terms of hygiene, cleanliness, food & nutrition and health related adjustment as compared to boys.

5.1.3d Social Adjustment

Table 5.1 further shows that adolescent girls (M = 4.66) scored higher on the mean score on social adjustment as compared to adolescent boys (M= 4.61) but the difference could not reach the level of significance (t =.285, n.s.).

5.1.3e School Adjustment

The mean score of adolescent girls (M = 4.61) is significantly (t = 2.66, p <.05) high on school adjustment as compared to adolescent boys (M= 4.22) as is presented in Table 5.1. The results shows that boys are better regulated in terms of their school adjustment as compared to girls.

Therefore, the hypothesis 1(d) that **"Adolescent boys will score significantly higher in terms of Emotional and School Adjustment as compared to adolescent girls"** stands proved and hypotheses 1(e) **"Adolescent girls will score significantly higher in terms of Family, Health and Social Adjustment as compared to adolescent boys"** is partially proved.

As is evident from the above results, it can be concluded that, the selected sample of boys are significantly better in terms of emotional and school adjustment whereas, girls are significantly better in health adjustment.

5.1.4 Academic Performance

Academic performance of the selected sample has been evaluated on the basis of the total academic grades secured in the final examination of the previous class attended The average of grade points obtained in five basic subject areas: Math, Science, English, Hindi and Social Studies. The grade scores for final data analysis for each student were obtained from the records of the school and were converted in to percentages.

The results of Academic Performance among adolescent boys and girls are presented in Table 5.1 and graphically depicted in Figure 5.1.

Table 5.1 indicates that mean score of adolescent girls (M = 78.03) is significantly (t = 4.59, p <.05) higher on Academic Performance as compared to adolescent boys (M= 72.76). The result depicts that girls have significantly higher level of academic performance as compared to boys. Therefore, the hypothesis **1(f)** that **"Adolescent girls will score significantly higher in terms of Academic Performance as compared to adolescent boys"** stands substantiated.

The girls have outscored boys in the academic arena which indicates that girls are more achievement oriented, better in their work and more focused in the completion of their task as compared to their male counterparts.

5.1.5 Parent Child Relationship

The Parent-Child Relationship Scale (PCRS) devised by Nalini Rao (1989) was administered on children to study the relationships of children with their parents. This tool contains 100 items categorized into ten dimensions namely: Protecting, Symbolic Punishment, Rejection, Object Punishment, Demanding, Indifferent, Symbolic Reward, Loving, Object Reward and Neglecting.

In the present study the scale was scored only for the mothers. The perceptions and experience of adolescents regarding their mothers' interaction with them was taken into consideration. The scores of boys and girls perception on the characteristic behavior of mothers as experienced by them were recorded as measure of Parent Child Relationship

The results of Parent-Child Relationship among adolescent boys and girls is presented in Table 5.1 and graphically depicted in Figure 5.1.Out of the ten variables of Parent-Child Relationship only two variables i.e. protecting and symbolic punishment showed significant difference in the mean scores of boys and girls.

5.1.5a Protecting

Table 5.1 clearly indicates that adolescent girls (M = 3.60) have significantly (t = -10.07, p <.05) scored higher on protecting dimension of Parent-Child Relationship as compared to adolescent boys (M= 2.65).Adolescent girls have higher scores on protecting dimension which signifies that girls perceive mothers to be more protective toward them.

5.1.5b Symbolic punishment

Furthermore, the mean score of adolescent boys (M = 3.64) is significantly (t = 15.47, p <.05) higher on symbolic punishment as compared to adolescent girls(M= 2.36) as is presented in Table 5.1. It clearly shows that boys feel that they get more punishment from their mothers.

5.1.5cRejection

Table 5.1 shows that adolescent boys (M = 3.40) scored higher on the dimension of rejection as compared to adolescent girls (M= 3.30) but the difference could not reach the level of significance (t =1.07, n.s.).

5.1.5dObject Punishment

The mean score of adolescent boys (M = 3.33) is higher on object punishment as compared to adolescent girls (M =3.32) as is presented in Table 5.1.But the difference failed to reach the level of significance (t =.125, n.s.).

5.1.5eDemanding

Table 5.1 shows that adolescent boys (M = 3.26) scored higher on the domain of rejection as compared to adolescent girls (M= 3.25) but the difference between the two groups was not significant (t =.040, n.s.).

5.1.5f Indifferent

The mean score of adolescent girls (M = 3.47) is higher on indifferent domain of Parent-Child Relationship as compared to adolescent boys (M =3.44) as is presented in Table 5.1.But the difference between boys and girls could not reach the level of significance (t =.391, n.s.).

5.1.5gSymbolic Reward

Furthermore, the mean score of adolescent boys (M = 3.36) is higher on symbolic reward as compared to adolescent girls (M= 3.34) as is evident from Table 5.1, but the difference failed to reach the level of significance (t =.257, n.s.).

5.1.5hLoving

As is depicted in Table 5.1that adolescent girls (M = 3.38) scored higher on the mean score on loving as compared to adolescent boys (M= 3.37) but the difference between boys and girls could not reach the level of significance (t =.083, n.s.).

5.1.5iObject Reward

The mean score of adolescent girls (M = 3.44) is higher on object reward as compared to adolescent boys (M =3.34) as is shown in Table 5.1.But the difference between the two could not reach the level of significance (t =.971, n.s.).

5.1.5j Neglecting

Further, Table 5.1 shows that adolescent girls (M = 3.44) scored higher on the domain of loving as compared to adolescent boys (M= 3.38) but the difference was not significant (t =.678, n.s.).

Therefore, the hypothesis **1(g)** that **"Adolescent girls will score significantly higher regarding their perception on Protecting and Loving dimension of Parent-Child Relationship (mothers) as compared to adolescent boys"** and hypotheses **1(h)** that **"Adolescent boys will score significantly higher regarding their perception on Symbolic Punishment and Symbolic Reward dimension of Parent-Child Relationship (mothers) as compared to adolescent girls"** stands partially proved.

Hence, it can be concluded from the above presented preliminary results that girls significantly outscored boys in the protecting dimension of Parent-Child Relationship which shows that girls find mothers to be more protecting towards them as compared to their male counterparts. On the other hand, boys significantly outscored girls on symbolic punishment which shows that boys perceive that mothers subject them to more symbolic punishment as compared to girls.

It can be summed from the results of the present investigation that boys in the state of Uttar Pradesh indulge in higher Internet communication than the adolescent girls. Nevertheless, girls have significantly higher general positive affect, emotional ties and life satisfaction whereas boys have significantly higher loss of behavioral/ emotional control. Interestingly, girls have also significantly higher level of depression as compared to boys.

Moreover, the boys have outscored girls on emotional and health dimensions of Psychosocial Adjustment as compared to girls which show that boys are significantly better regulated in their emotional and school adjustment. Girls have shown significantly better health adjustment than boys which shows girls are more health conscious than boys.

Furthermore, girls have higher academic performance than their male counterparts. It shows that adolescent girls have significantly better academic achievement than boys.

Lastly, on the dimensions of Parent-Child Relationship significant differences have emerged only on two dimensions i.e., protecting and symbolic punishment. Girls have perceived their mother to be higher on protecting dimension, whereas boys perceived that they get more symbolic punishment from their mothers.

Results of Correlation Analysis

In order to see the effect of internet communication on mental health, psycho social adjustment, academic performance and parent-child relationship among boys and girls correlation analysis was carried out. Intercorrelation of Internet Addiction, Internet Usage and Internet Attitude with Mental Health, Psychosocial Adjustment, Academic Performance and Parent-Child Relationship are presented separately for boys and girls in Table 5.2 and Table 5.3, respectively.

5.2 INTERCORRELATION OF INTERNET COMMUNICATION (INTERNET ADDICTION, INTERNET USAGE AND INTERNET ATTITUDE), MENTAL HEALTH, ACADEMIC PERFORMANCE, PSYCHOSOCIAL ADJUSTMENT AND PARENT-CHILD RELATIONSHIP AMONG ADOLESCENT BOYS

Intercorrelation of Internet Addiction, Internet Usage and Internet Attitude, six variables of Mental Health (Anxiety, Depression, Loss of Behavioral / Emotional Control, General Positive Affect, Emotional Ties and Life Satisfaction), five variables of Psychosocial adjustment(emotional, family, health, school and social), Academic Performance and ten dimensions of Parent-Child Relationship (Protecting, Symbolic Punishment, Rejection, Object Punishment, Demanding, Indifferent, Symbolic Reward, Loving, Object Reward and Neglecting) among adolescent boys is presented in Table 5.2.

5.2.1 Internet Addiction

5.2.1a Intercorrelation of Internet Addiction and Mental Health among Boys

Internet addiction was measured among adolescent boys with the help of Internet Addiction Test (Young 1996) and the results are presented herein. Table 5.2 reveals that there is a positive and significant relationship ($r = .711$, $p < .01$) between Internet Addiction and Anxiety which clearly shows that higher the Internet Addiction higher is the Anxiety among adolescent boys. It indicates that higher internet addiction leads to nervousness, anxiousness, agitation, uneasiness and makes them fearful.

Table 5.2 reveals that there is a positive and significant correlation ($r =. 362$, $p < .01$) between Internet Addiction and Depression which clearly shows that higher the Internet Addiction higher is the Depression among adolescent boys,which indicates that excessive use of Internetmakes the boys sad, unhappy and dejected.

The perusal results indicates that there is a positive and significant correlation ($r = .377$, $p < .01$) between Internet Addiction and Loss of Behavioral and Emotional Control presented in Table 5.2. It depicts that higher the Internet Addiction higher is the Loss of Behavioral and Emotional Control among adolescent boys.

It is also evident from Table 5.2 that there is a negative and significant relationship ($r = -.366$, $p < .01$) between Internet Addiction and General Positive Affect among boys which clearly shows that higher the Internet Addiction lesser is the General Positive Affect among the selected sample of boys.

Furthermore, the results indicate that there is a negative and significant correlation ($r = -.262$, $p < .01$) between Internet Addiction and Emotional Ties shown in Table 5.2.It signifies that higher the Internet Addiction lesser are the Emotional Ties among adolescent boys.

It is also evident from Table 5.2 that there is a significant and negative correlation ($r = -.282$, $p < .01$) between Internet Addiction and Life Satisfaction. The result indicates higher the Internet Addiction lesser is the Life Satisfaction among adolescent boys.

In sum, the above results depict that Internet Addiction is significantly and positively related to Anxiety, Depression, and Loss of Behavioral/Emotional control among adolescent boys. On the contrary, Internet Addiction is negatively and significantly related to General Positive Affect, Emotional Ties and Life Satisfaction among adolescent boys.

Thus, the results partially substantiate hypothesis **2(a) "Internet Addiction will be significantly and positively related to Anxiety, Depression, loss of Behavioral/Emotional control among adolescent boys"** and hypotheses **2(b) "Internet Addiction will be significantly and negatively related to General Positive Affect, Emotional Ties and Life Satisfaction among adolescent boys"**stands proved.

Table 5.2: Showing Intercorrelation of Internet Communication (Internet Addiction, Internet Usage andInternet Attitude), six sub Variables of Mental Health, Five Variables of Psychosocial Adjustment, Academic Performance and ten variables of Parent-Child Relationship among Adolescent Boys

Sr. No.	Variables	Internet Communication		
		Internet Addiction	Internet Usage	Internet Attitude
1.	**Mental Health**			
1	Anxiety	.711**	.411**	.332**
2	Depression	.362**	.469**	.270**
3	Loss of Behavioural/ Emotional control	.377**	.042	.316**
4	General Positive Affect	-.366**	-.083	-.209**
5	Emotional Ties	-.262**	.020	-.275**
6	Life Satisfaction	-.282**	.009	-.244**
2.	**Psychosocial Adjustment**			
1	Emotional	.434**	.181**	.296**
2	Family	-.317**	-.230**	-.107
3	Health	.652**	.424**	.341**
4	Social	.735**	.355**	.356**
5	School	.062	.101	-.020
3.	**Academic Performance**	-.338**	-.091	-.192**
4.	**Parent Child Relationship**			
1	Protecting	.537**	.247**	.277**
2	Symbolic Punishment	.413**	.279**	.168**
3	Rejection	-.068	-.087	-.083
4	Object Punishment	-.039	-.011	-.048
5	Demanding	.057	.016	.054
6	Indifferent	.040	-.035	-.066
7	Symbolic Reward	-.044	.014	-.072
8	Loving	-.012	-.009	.010
9	Object Reward	.006	.027	.048

10	Neglecting		-.051	.012	-.130*

*p<.05, **p<.01

5.2.1b   Intercorrelation of Internet Addiction and Psychosocial Adjustment among Boys

Psychosocial adjustment among the selected sample of adolescents was measured using the Psychosocial Adjustment Scale (Global Adjustment Scale, Form –S, Psycom Services, 1994). High scores on the five domains of the scale have to be interpreted as low adjustment per the scoring instructions of the scale.

Table 5.2 reveals that there is a significant and positive correlation (r = .434, p <.01) between Internet Addiction and Emotional Adjustment. It shows that higher Internet Addiction leads to poor Emotional Adjustment among boys.

Furthermore, Table 5.2 indicates that there is a significant and negative correlation (r = -.317, p <.01) between Internet Addiction and Family Adjustment. It reveals that higher internet addiction leads to better Family Adjustment among adolescent boys.

It is also evident from Table 5.2 there is a positive and significant correlation (r = .652, p <.01) between Internet Addiction and Health Adjustment, which showsthat higher Internet Addiction leads to poor Health Adjustment among selected sample of boys.

Moreover, Table 5.2 indicates that there is apositive and significant correlation (r =.735, p <.01) between Internet Addiction and Social Adjustment, higher the Internet Addiction lower is the Social Adjustment among adolescent boys. There is an adverse impact of Internet Addiction on Social Adjustment among boys. Therefore, the hypothesis **3(a)** that **"Internet Addiction will be significantly and positively related to Emotional, Family, Health, Social and School Adjustment of adolescent boys"** is partially proved.

5.2.1c Intercorrelation of Internet Addiction and Academic Performance among Boys

Table 5.2 clearly reveals that there exists a negative and significant correlation (r = -.338, p <.01) between Internet Addiction and Academic Performance which clearly indicates that higher the Internet Addiction poor is the Academic Performance. The results indicate that boys who are addicted to internet are poor in their school, academic and scholastic performance. Thus, the hypothesis **4(a)** that **"Internet Addiction will be significantly and negatively related to the Academic Performance of adolescent boys"** stands proved.

5.2.1d   Intercorrelation of Internet Addiction and Parent-Child Relationship among Boys

Internet Addiction has a significant positive correlation ($r = .537$, $p < .01$) with the Protecting dimension of Parent-Child Relationship as is presented in Table 5.2. It signifies that higher the Internet Addiction higher the boys have perceived their mothers to be more protective.

It is also evident from Table 5.2 that there is asignificantand positive correlation ($r = .413$, $p < .01$) between Internet Addiction and Symbolic Punishment which indicates higher the Internet Addiction higher is the Symbolic Punishment from the mothers towards adolescent boys. Hence, the results partially substantiate hypothesis **5(a)** that **"Internet Addiction will be significantly and positively related to Protecting, Symbolic Punishment, Rejecting and Object Punishment dimension of Parent-Child Relationship (mothers) among adolescent boys"** andhypotheses **5(b)** **"Internet Addiction will be significantly and negatively related to Loving dimension of Parent-Child Relationship (mothers) among adolescent boys"** is not proved.

It can be concluded from the above mentioned results that Internet Addiction has a negative impact on the mental health of boys. It shows that internet addiction leads to mental health problems like anxiety, depression and loss of behavioral/emotional problems among boys. Depression is the most frequently reported psychiatric symptom associated with Internet addiction. Internet Addiction has a significant negative impact on the general positive affect, emotional ties, and life satisfaction among boys which shows that higher the internet addiction poor is the mental health.

Furthermore, Internet Addiction also has significant negative impact on the emotional, health and social adjustment among boys. This shows that higher internet addiction leads to poor adjustment among boys. Surprisingly, the results indicate that Internet Addiction leads to better family adjustment among boys.

Moreover, Internet addiction also has a negative impact on the academic performance of boys. It shows that boys who are addicted to internet are having poor academic performance.

Lastly, Parent-Child Relationship was found to be strongly associated with adolescents' Internet addiction tendency. Boys who are addicted to Internet perceived their mothers to be giving them more symbolic punishment and perceive them to be more protective towards them.

5.2.2 Internet Usage

5.2.2a Intercorrelation of Internet Usage and Mental Health among adolescent Boys

Table 5.2 indicates that there is a positive and significant correlation ($r = .411$, $p<.01$) between Internet Usage and Anxiety which clearly shows that higher the internet usage higher is the level of anxiety among the selected sample of boys. Hence, the higher Internet usage among adolescent boys leads to more anxiety among them.

It is also evident from Table 5.2 that there exists a positive and significant relationship ($r = .469$, $p <.01$) between Internet Usage and Depression which clearly shows that higher the internet usage higher is the depression among adolescent boys.

Above results indicate that higher Internet Usage significantly increase the anxiety and depression among adolescent boys. Thus, the results substantiate the hypothesis **2(e)** that **"Internet Usage will be significantly and positively related to Anxiety and Depression among adolescent boys".**

5.2.2b Intercorrelation of Internet Usage and Psychosocial Adjustment among Boys

As per the scoring instructions of the scale high scores have to be interpreted as poor adjustment.

Table 5.2 indicates a significant and positive correlation ($r = .181$, $p <.01$) between Internet Usage and Emotional Adjustment, which clearly shows that higher the internet addiction poor is the emotional adjustment among selected sample of boys.

Further, Table 5.2 shows that there is a significant and negative correlation ($r = -.230$, $p <.01$) between Internet Usage and Family Adjustment among adolescent boys which reveals that higher the internet usage better is the family adjustment among boys.

It is also evident from Table 5.2 that there is a significant positive correlation ($r = .424$, $p <.01$) between Internet Usage and Health Adjustment, which clearly depicts that higher the internet addiction poor is the health adjustment among adolescent boys.

As is evident from Table 5.2 that there is a significant positive correlation (r = .355, p <.01) between Internet Usage and Social Adjustment. This indicates that higher the internet addiction poor is the social adjustment among the selected sample of boys.

5.2.2c Intercorrelation of Internet Usage and Academic Performance among Boys

Table 5.2 indicates a negative and significant correlation (r = -.205, p <.01) between Internet Usage and Academic Performance, which clearly shows that higher the internet addiction poor is the academic performance among adolescent boys. Thus, the results substantiate hypothesis **4 (c)** that **"Internet Usage will be significantly and negatively related to Academic Performance of adolescent boys"**. The intercorrelation shows that higher usage of internet adversely affects the academic accomplishment among adolescent boys.

5.2.2d Intercorrelation of Internet Usage and Parent-Child Relationship among Boys

It is also evident from the Table 5.2 that there is a positive and significant relationship (r = .247, p <.01) between Internet Usage and Protecting dimension of Parent Child Relationship. This clearly indicates that higher the Internet usage higher the boys have perceived their mothers to be over protective.

It is also evident from the Table 5.2 that there is a positive and significant relationship (r = .279, p <.01) between Internet Usage and Symbolic Punishment. This shows that higher the internet usage higher is the boys' perception that their mothers subject them to more symbolic punishment.

Thus, it is obvious from above mentioned results that Internet Usage has a significant negative impact on anxiety and depression among boys. This shows that boys who are prone to excessive internet usage are more anxious and depressed in their lives. Higher internet usage has a detrimental effect on their mental health.

Moreover, Internet Usage also has a significant negative impact on the emotional, health and social adjustment among boys.But surprisingly Internet Usage leads to better family adjustment among them. This shows that excessive internet usage leads to poor emotional, health and social adjustment at the same time internet usage leads to better family adjustment among boys.

Furthermore, Internet Usage has a negative impact on the academic performance of boys. It shows excessive use of internet leads to poor academic performance among boys.

Lastly, boys who are prone to excessive Internet usage have perceived their mothers to be giving them more symbolic punishment and they perceived their mothers to be more protective towards them.

5.2.3Internet Attitude

5.2.3a Intercorrelation of Internet Attitude and Mental Health among Boys

It is evident from Table 5.2 that there is a positive and significant correlation ($r = .332$, $p < .01$) between Internet Attitude and Anxiety which clearly shows that higher the internet attitude higher is the anxiety among adolescent boys.

Likewise, Table 5.2 indicates that there isa positive and significant correlation($r = .316$, $p < .01$) between Internet Attitude and Loss of Behavioral and Emotional Control, which indicates that higher the Internet Attitude higher is the loss of behavioral and emotional control amongboys. Higher Internet Attitude adversely affects the behavioral and emotional control among boys.

It is also evident from Table 5.2 that there exist a negative and significant correlation ($r = -.209$, $p < .01$) between Internet Attitude and General Positive Affect among adolescent boys which indicates that higher the Internet Attitude lesser is the General Positive Affect among boys. Higher Internet Attitude of boys decreases the general positive affect among them.

Furthermore, Table 5.2 indicates that there is a negative and significant correlation ($r = -.275$, $p < .01$) between Internet Attitude and Emotional Ties. The result signifies that higher Internet Attitude adversely effects the emotional ties among boys.

It is also evident from Table 5.2 that there is a positive and significant correlation ($r = -.244$, $p < .01$) between Internet Attitude and life satisfaction. It indicates that higher the internet Attitude lesser is the life satisfaction among adolescent boys.

5.2.3b Intercorrelation of Internet Attitude and Psychosocial Adjustment among Boys

As per the scoring instructions of the scale high scores have to be interpreted as poor adjustment.

Table 5.2 indicates that there is a significant and positive correlation ($r = .296$, $p < .01$) between Internet attitude and Emotional Adjustment which clearly depicts that higher the internet addiction poor is the emotional adjustment among adolescent boys. The Intercorrelation shows that there is an adverse impact of internet attitude which affects the emotional adjustment among boys.

It is also evident from Table 5.2 that there is a significant negative correlation ($r = -.107$, $p < .01$) between Internet Attitude and Family Adjustment among boys. This indicates that higher internet attitude leads to better family adjustment among the selected sample of boys.

Further, Table 5.2 indicates that there is a significant and positive correlation ($r = .341$, $p < .01$) between Internet Attitude and Health Adjustment, which reveals that higher the internet attitude poor is the health adjustment among adolescent boys.

It is also evident from Table 5.2 that there is a significant and negative correlation ($r = .356$, $p < .01$) between Internet Attitude and Social Adjustment. It shows that higher the internet attitude poor is the social adjustment among the selected sample of boys.

5.2.3c Intercorrelation of Internet Attitude and Academic Performance among Boys

Table 5.2 clearly indicates that there is a negative and significant correlation ($r = -.192$, $p < .01$) between Internet Attitude and Academic Performance which signifies that higher the internet attitude poor is the Academic Performance.

5.2.3d Intercorrelation of Internet Attitude and Parent-Child Relationship among Boys

It is evident from Table 5.2 that there is a positive and significant correlation ($r = .277$, $p < .01$) between Internet Attitude and Protecting dimension of Parent Child Relationship. This clearly signifies that higher the internet attitude higher is the perception among boys that mothers are protective towards them.

The Table 5.2 also reveals that there is a positive and significant correlation ($r = .168$, $p < .01$) between Internet Attitude and Symbolic Punishment. The results indicate that higher the internet attitude higher is the symbolic punishment perceived by the boys from their mothers.

Furthermore, it is evident from Table 5.2 that there is a negative and significant correlation ($r = -.130$, $p < .01$) between Internet Attitude and Neglecting dimension of Parent Child Relationship. It signifies that higher the internet attitude more the boys perceive their mothers to be neglecting towards them.

In sum, the above results indicate that Internet Attitude has a negative impact on the mental health of boys. It shows that higher internet attitude leads to mental health problems like anxiety, loss of behavioral/emotional control. It leads to poor general positive affect, emotional ties, and life satisfaction among boys which shows that higher the internet attitude poor is the mental health.

Furthermore, Internet Attitude also has significant negative impact on the emotional, health and social adjustment among boys. Surprisingly, higher internet attitude leads to better family adjustment among boys. This shows that higher internet attitude leads to poor adjustment among boys accept family adjustment.

Moreover, higher Internet attitude has a negative impact on the academic performance of boys. The results indicate that boys who are having higher internet attitude are not performing well in their academics.

Lastly, boys who are having higher internet attitude perceived their mothers to be giving them more symbolic punishment and perceived their mothers to be having neglecting approach towards them.

5.3 CORRELATION OF INTERNET COMMUNICATION (INTERNET ADDICTION, INTERNET USAGE AND INTERNET ATTITUDE), MENTAL HEALTH, ACADEMIC PERFORMANCE, PSYCHOSOCIAL ADJUSTMENT AND PARENT-CHILD RELATIONSHIP AMONG ADOLESCENT GIRLS

Intercorrelation of Internet Addiction, Internet Usage and Internet Attitude with six variables of Mental Health (Anxiety, Depression, Loss of Behavioral / Emotional Control, General Positive Affect, Emotional Ties and Life Satisfaction), five variables of Psychosocial Adjustment(Emotional, Family, Health, Schooland social),Academic Performance and ten dimensions of Parent-Child Relationship (Protecting, Symbolic Punishment, Rejection, Object

Punishment, Demanding, Indifferent, Symbolic Reward, Loving, Object Reward and Neglecting) among adolescent girls is presented in Table 5.3.

5.3.1 Internet Addiction

5.3.1a Intercorrelation of Internet Addiction and Mental Health among Girls

It is evident from Table 5.3 that there is a positive and significant correlation ($r = .298$, p <.01) between Internet Addiction and Depression which clearly shows that higher internet addiction leads to higher depression among adolescent girls.Further, Table 5.3 indicates that there is a positive and significant correlation ($r = .298$, p <.01) between Internet Addiction and Loss of Behavioral and Emotional Control, which clearly shows that higher the Internet addiction higher isthe loss of behavioral and emotional control among adolescent girls.

It is also evident from Table 5.3 that there is a negative and significant relationship ($r = -.293$, p <.01) between Internet Addiction and General Positive Affect among adolescent girls which reveals that higher the internet addiction lesser is the general positive affect among the selected sample of girls.

Further, the Table indicates that there is a negative and significant correlation ($r = -.266$, p <.01) between Internet Addiction and Emotional Ties, which signifies that higher Internet addiction leads to poor emotional ties among adolescent girls.

It is also evident from Table 5.3 that there is a negative and significant correlation ($r = -.360$, p <.01) between Internet Addiction and Life Satisfaction. This reveals that higher internet addiction leads to poor life satisfaction among adolescent girls. Thus, the results partially substantiate the hypothesis that **2(b) "Internet Addiction will be significantly and positively related to Anxiety, Depression, Loss of Behavioral/Emotional control among adolescent girls"** and hypotheses2(c)that **"Internet Addiction will be significantly and negatively related to General Positive Affect, Emotional Ties and Life Satisfaction among adolescent girls"** is partially proved.

5.3.1b Intercorrelation of Internet Addiction and Psychosocial Adjustment among Girls

As per the scoring instructions of the scale high scores have to be interpreted as poor adjustment.

It is evident from Table 5.3 that there is a positive and significant correlation ($r = .333$, p <.01) between Internet Addition and Emotional Adjustment. It signifies that higher Internet addiction leads to poor emotional adjustment among girls.

Further, the Table indicates that there is a negative and significant correlation ($r = -.309$, p <.01) between Internet Addition and Family Adjustment, which shows that higherInternet addiction leads to better family adjustment among girls.

It is also evident from Table 5.3 that there is a positive and significant correlation ($r = .544$, p <.01) between Internet Addition and Health Adjustment, which reveals that higher Internet addiction among girls leads to poor health adjustment among them.

Further, Table 5.3 indicates that there is positive and significant correlation ($r = .524$, p <.01) between Internet Addition and Social Adjustment, which shows that higher the internet addiction poor is the social adjustment among girls. Therefore, the hypotheses that **3(b)** that **"Internet Addiction will be significantly and positively related to Emotional, Family, Health, Social and School Adjustment of adolescent girls"** ispartially proved.

5.3.1c Intercorrelation of Internet Addiction and Academic Performance among Girls

Table 5.3 clearly indicates that there is a negative and significant correlation ($r = -.371$, p <.01) between Internet Addiction and Academic Performance among girls which reveals that higher the internet addiction poor is their academic achievement. Thus, the hypotheses that **4(c)** **"Internet Addiction will be significantly and negatively related to Academic Performance of adolescent girls"** stands proved.

Table 5.3: Showing Correlation of Internet Communication (Internet Addiction, Internet Usage and Internet Attitude), six sub Variables of Mental Health, Five Variables of Psychosocial Adjustment, Academic Performance and ten variables Parent-Child Relationship among Adolescent Girls

Sr. No.	Variables	Internet communication		
		Internet Addiction	Internet Usage	Internet Attitude
	Mental Health			
1.	Anxiety	.018	-.001	.043
2	Depression	.298**	.441**	.065
3	Loss of Behavioural/Emotional control	.541**	.297**	.103
4	General Positive Affect	-.293**	-.094	-.127*
5	Emotional Ties	-.266**	.001	-.108
6	Life Satisfaction	-.360**	.005	-.076
2.	**Psychosocial Adjustment**			
1	Emotional	.333**	.143*	.096
2	Family	-.309**	-.179**	-.126*
3	Health	.544**	.310**	.135*
4	Social	.524**	.196**	.168**
5	School	-.010	-.023	.040
3.	**Academic Performance**	-.371**	-.205**	-.186**
4.	**Parent Child Relationship**			
1	Protecting	.173**	.088	.074
2	Symbolic Punishment	.537**	.279**	.097
3	Rejection	.043	.049	-.050
4	Object Punishment	.084	-.009	.129*
5	Demanding	-.024	-.049	-.043
6	Indifferent	.043	-.053	.058
7	Symbolic Reward	-.047	-.011	-.032
8	Loving	.059	.020	-.014
9	Object Reward	.044	-.009	.053

| 10 | Neglecting | -.061 | .078 | .046 |

*p<.05, **p<.01

5.3.1d   Intercorrelation of Internet Addiction and Parent-Child Relationship among Girls

It is also evident from Table 5.3 that there is a positive and significant correlation (r = .173, p <.01) between Internet Addiction and Protecting dimension of Parent Child Relationship. This signifies that higher the Internet addiction higher is the protection from mother as perceived by adolescent girls.

It is also evident from Table 5.3 that there is a positive and significant correlation (r = .537, p <.01) between Internet Addiction and Symbolic Punishment. This indicates that higher Internet addiction will lead to higher symbolic punishment perceived by the adolescent girls from their mothers. Therefore, the hypotheses that **5(c)"Internet Addiction will be significantly and positively related toProtecting, Symbolic Punishment, Rejecting and Object Punishment dimension of Parent-Child Relationship among adolescent girls"** partially corroborate and hypothesesthat **5(d)"Internet Addiction will be significantly and negatively related to Loving dimension of Parent-Child Relationship among adolescent girls"** is not proved.

Thus, the above mentioned results show that Internet Addiction has a negative impact on the mental health of girls. Internet addiction leads to mental health problems like depression, loss of behavioral/emotional problems and it also leads to poor general positive affect, emotional ties, and life satisfaction among girls.Higher internet addiction leads to psychological distress among girls.

Furthermore, Internet addiction leads to poor emotional, health and social adjustment among girls. Surprisingly, in case of girls also higher internet addiction leads to better family adjustment.

Moreover, Internet addiction also has a negative impact on the academic performance of girls. It shows that girls who are addicted to internet are having poor academic performance.

Lastly, girls who are addicted to Internet perceived their mothers to be giving them more symbolic punishment. Apart from that girls who are addicted to internet perceived their mothers to be over protective and they are more prone towards Internet addiction.

5.3.2 Internet Usage

5.3.2a Intercorrelation of Internet Usage and Mental Health among Girls

As is evident from Table 5.3 that there is a positive and significant correlation ($r = .441$, p <.01) between Internet Usage and Depression which shows that higher the internet usage higher is the depression among adolescent girls.

Table 5.3 further shows that there is a positive and significant correlation ($r = .297$, p <.01) between Internet Usage and Loss of Behavioral and Emotional Control which indicates that higher the internet usage higher is the loss of behavioral and emotional control among adolescent girls. Therefore, the hypotheses **2(f) "Internet Usage will be significantly and positively related to Anxiety and Depression among adolescent girls"** is partially proved.

5.3.2b Intercorrelation of Internet Usage and Psychosocial Adjustment among Girls

As per the scoring instructions of the scale high scores have to be interpreted as poor adjustment.

Further the Table 5.3 indicates that there is a positive and significant correlation ($r = .143$, p <.01) between Internet Usage and Emotional Adjustment, which reveals that higher the internet addiction poor is the emotional adjustment among adolescent girls. It is also evident from Table 5.3 that there is a negative and significant correlation ($r = -.179$, p <.01) between Internet Usage and Family Adjustment among adolescent girls which indicates that higher the internet usage better is the family adjustment among adolescent girls.

Furthermore, Table 5.3 indicates that there is a positive and significant correlation ($r = .310$, p <.01) between Internet Usage and Health Adjustment, which shows that higher the internet addiction poor is the health adjustment among adolescent girls. It is also evident from Table 5.3 that there is a negative and significant correlation ($r = .196$, p <.01) between Internet

Usage and Social Adjustment. This signifies that higher internet addiction leads to poor social adjustment among adolescent girls.

5.3.2c Intercorrelation of Internet Usage and Academic Performance among Girls

Table 5.3 indicates that there is a significant negative correlation (r = -.205, p <.01) between Internet Usage and Academic Performance which reveals that higher the Internet addiction, poor will be the Academic Achievement among girls. Therefore, the hypothesis **4(d)** **"Internet Usage will be significantly and negatively related to Academic Performance of adolescent girls"** is corroborated.

5.3.2d Intercorrelation of Internet Usage and Parent-Child Relationship among Girls

Table 5.3 indicates that there is a significant positive correlation (r = .279, p <.01) between Internet Usage and Symbolic Punishment dimension of Parent Child Relationship. This signifies that higher internet usage leads to higher symbolic punishment as perceived by the girls from their mothers.

It is concluded from the above mentioned results that the Internet Usage has a significant negative impact on the mental health, specifically; it leads to depression and loss of behavioral/emotional control among girls.

Moreover, Internet Usage also has significant negative impact on the emotional, health and social adjustment among girls. But Internet usage leads to better family adjustment among them.

Furthermore, Internet usage has a negative impact on the academic performance of girls. It shows excessive use of Internet leads to poor academic performance among girls.

Lastly, girls who are prone to excessive Internet usage have perceived their mothers to be giving them more symbolic punishment.

5.3.3 Internet Attitude

5.3.3a Intercorrelation of Internet Attitude and Mental Health among Girls

Table 5.3 reveals that there exists a significant negative correlation (r = -.127, p <.01) between Internet Attitude and General Positive Affect among adolescent girls which shows that higher the internet Attitude lesser is the general positive affect among adolescent girls. None of the other five variables of mental health have a significant correlation with internet attitude.

5.3.3b Intercorrelation of Internet Attitude and Psychosocial Adjustment among Girls

As per the scoring instructions of the scale high scores have to be interpreted as poor adjustment.

It is also evident from Table 5.3 that there is a significant negative correlation (r = -.126, p <.01) between Internet Attitude and Family Adjustment among adolescent girls which shows that higher internet attitude leads to better family adjustment among adolescent girls.

Further, Table 5.3 indicates that there is a significant positive correlation (r = .135, p <.01) between Internet Attitude and Health Adjustment, which reveals that higher the internet attitude poor is the health adjustment among girls.

It is also evident from Table 5.3 that there is a significant positive correlation (r = .168, p <.01) between Internet Attitude and Social Adjustment. This signifies that higher the internet attitude poor is the social adjustment among girls.

5.3.3c Intercorrelation of Internet Attitude and Academic Performance among adolescent girls

Table 5.3 clearly indicates that there is a significant negative correlation (r = -.186, p <.01) between Internet Attitude and Academic Performance which shows that higher Internet attitude leads to poor academic performance among the selected girls.

5.3.3d Intercorrelation of Internet Attitude and Parent-Child Relationship among Girls

Table 5.3 indicates that there is a significant positive correlation (r = .129, p <.05) between Internet Attitude and Object Punishment. This shows that higher internet attitude leads to higher object punishment perceived by girls from their mothers.

In sum, the above results indicate that Internet Attitude has a negative impact on general positive affect among girls. Furthermore, higher Internet Attitude leads to poor health and social adjustment among girls. But higher internet attitude leads to better family adjustment among them.

Moreover, higher Internet attitude has a negative impact on the academic performance of girls. Girls who are having higher Internet attitude are not performing well in their academics.

Lastly, girls who are having higher internet attitude perceived their mothers to be subjecting them to more object punishment.

Regression Analysis

In order to identify the significant predictors of Mental Health, Psychosocial Adjustment and Academic Performance, stepwise regression analysis was carried out for all the predicted variables separately for boys and girls. The predictor variables included Internet Communication (Internet Addiction, Internet Usage and Internet Attitude) and ten dimensions of Parent-Child Relationship (Protecting, Symbolic Punishment, Rejection, Object Punishment, Demanding, Indifferent, Symbolic Reward, Loving, Object Reward and Neglecting)

5.4 STEPWISE MULTIPLE REGRESSION ANALYSIS OF INTERNET COMMUNICATION AND PARENT-CHILD RELATIONSHIP AS PREDICTORS OF MENTAL HEALTH AMONG BOYS AND GIRLS

5.4.1aAnxiety

The result of stepwise regression analysis of Internet Communication and Parent-Child Relationship as Predictors of Anxiety among adolescent boys and girls is presented in Table 5.4 and Table 5.5, respectively.

Table 5.4: Stepwise Regression Analysis of Internet Communication and Parent-Child Relationship as Predictors of Anxiety among Adolescent Boys

Independent variable	r	Beta Coefficient	t	R^2	R^2Change	F-Value (R^2Change)
InternetAddiction	.711**	.700	15.456**	.491	.491	238.903**

**p<.01; *p<.05

Table 5.4 reveals that the significant predictor variable of Anxiety among adolescent boys was Internet Addiction (β = .700, t = 15.45, p <.01). Thus, higher Anxiety among boys was predicted by higher Internet addiction. This variable accounted for 49.1 per cent (F= 238.90, p< .01) of the variance in the Internet Addiction of the adolescent boys.

Table 5.5: **Stepwise Regression Analysis of Internet Communication and Parent- Child Relationship as Predictors of Anxiety among Adolescent Girls**

Independent variable	r	Beta Coefficient	t	R^2	R^2Change	F-Value (R^2 Change)
Internet Addiction	.018	.159	2.539**	.025	.025	6.446**

**p<.01; *p<.05

It is evident from Table 5.5 that the only significant predictor variable of Anxiety among adolescent girls was Internet Addiction (β =.159, t = 2.539, p <.01).Higher internet addiction leads to higher anxiety. This variable accounted for 2.5 per cent (F= 6.446, p< .05) of the variance in the internet scores of the adolescent girls.

It is noteworthy that Internet Addiction emerged as the most significant predictor of Anxiety among both adolescent boys and girls. The results indicate that the more addictive to the Internet a student is, the more anxiety he/she experiences.

5.4.1b Depression

The result of stepwise regression analysis of Internet Communication and Parent-Child Relationship as Predictors of Depression among adolescent boys and girls is presented in Table 5.6 and Table 5.7, respectively.

Table 5.6: **Stepwise Regression Analysis of Internet Communication and Parent-Child Relationship as Predictors of Depression among Adolescent Boys**

IndependentVariable	r	Beta Coefficient	t	R^2	R^2Change	F-Value (R^2 Change)
Internet Usage	.469**	.504	9.189**	.254	.254	84.435**
Internet Addiction	.362**	.262	4.049**	.300	.046	16.395**

**p<.01 and *p<.05

Table 5.6 reveals that the significant predictor variables of Depression among boys were Internet Usage (β = .504, t = 9.189, p <.01) and Internet Addiction (β =.26, t = 4.049, p <.01).

Thus, the higher Depression among boys was predicted by higher Internet Usage and higher Internet Addiction. These two variables accounted for 30 per cent of variance in the Depression of the adolescent boys. Out of this, the Internet Usage explained 25.4 per cent (F= 84.435, p< .01) of the variance and Internet Addiction explained an additional 4.6 per cent (F = 16.395, P<.01) of the variance in the depression of the adolescent boys.

Table 5.7: Stepwise Regression Analysis of Internet Communication and Parent- Child Relationship as Predictors of Depression among Adolescent Girls

Independent variable	r	Beta Coefficient	t	R^2	R^2Change	F-Value (R^2 Change)
Internet Usage	.441**	.441	7.734**	.194	.194	59.808**
Internet Addiction	.298**	.161	2.575**	.232	.021	6.633**
Protecting	-.092	-.132	2.319**	.211	.017	5.378**

**p<.01; *p<.05

Table 5.7 reveals that the significant predictor variables of Depression among adolescent girls were Internet Usage (β =.441, t = 7.734, p <.01), Protecting (β = -.132, t = 2.319, p <.01) and Internet Addiction (β = .16, t = 2.575, p <.01).

Thus, higher Depression was predicted by higher Internet Usage, Internet Addiction and Protecting among girls. These three variables were accounted for 23.2 per cent of variance in the Depression of the adolescent girls. Out of this, the Internet Usage explained 19.4 per cent (F= 59.808, p< .01) of the variance, Internet Addiction explained an additional 2.1 per cent (F = 6.633, P<.01) and Protection explained 1.7 per cent (F = 5.378 p< .01)of the variance in the Depression of the adolescent girls.

Therefore, it is obvious from above results that the significant predictors of Depression among both boys and girls were Internet Usage and Internet Addiction. But in case of girls, Protecting dimension of Parent-Child Relationship was also one of the variables which was creating Depression among them. These variables negatively influenced the depression among both boys and girls.

5.4.1c Loss of Behavioral/Emotional Control

The result of stepwise regression analysis of Internet Communication and Parent-Child Relationship as Predictors of Loss of Behavioral/Emotional control among adolescent boys and girls is presented in Table 5.8 and Table 5.9, respectively.

Table 5.8: Stepwise Regression Analysis of Internet Communication and Parent- Child Relationship as Predictors of Loss of Behavioral/Emotional Control among Adolescent Boys

Independent Variable	r	Beta Coefficient	t	R^2	R^2 Change	F-Value (R^2 Change)
Internet Addiction	.377**	.716	16.167**	.513	.513	261.372**
Internet Attitude	.316**	.150	3.101**	.531	.018	9.615**
Protecting	.430**	.122	2.410**	.54	.010	5.807**

**p<.01; *p<.05

Table 5.8 reveals that the significant predictor variables of Loss of Behavioral/Emotional Control among the adolescent boys was Internet Addiction (β =. 716, t= 16.167, p <.01), Internet Attitude (β =.150 and t = 3.101, p <.01), and Protecting (β =.122 and t = 2.410, p <.01). Thus, it shows that as Internet Addiction, Internet Attitude and Protecting dimension of Parent-Child Relationship increases, the Loss of Behavioral/Emotional Control among boys also increases.

The higher Loss of Behavioral /Emotional Control among boys were predicted by higher Internet Addiction, Internet Attitude and Protecting dimension of Parent Child Relationship. These three variables accounted for 54.1 per cent of variance in the Loss of Behavioral/Emotional Control of the adolescent boys. Out of this, the Internet Addiction explained 51.3 per cent (F= 261.372, p< .01) of the variance, Internet Attitude explained remaining an additional 1.8 per cent (F = 9.615, P<.01) and Protecting explained remaining 1.0 per cent (F = 5.807, P<.01) of the variance in the Loss of Behavioral/Emotional Control of the adolescent boys.

Table 5.9: **Stepwise Regression Analysis of Internet Communication and Parent- Child Relationship as Predictors of Loss of Behavioral/Emotional Control among Adolescent Girls**

Independent variable	r	Beta Coefficient	t	R^2	R^2Change	F- Value (R^2Change)
Internet Addiction	.541**	.660	13.827**	.435	.435	191.193**

**p<.01; *p<.05

It is evident from Table 5.9 that the only significant predictor variables of Loss of Behavioral/Emotional Control among adolescent girls was Internet Addiction (β =.660, t = 13.827, p <.01).

Thus, higher Loss of Behavioral/Emotional Control among girls was predicted by higher Internet Addiction. This variable accounted for 43.5 per cent(F= 191.193, p< .01) of the variance in the Loss of Behavioral/Emotional Control of the adolescent girls.

It is noteworthy from the above results that the significant predictors of Loss of Behavioral/Emotional Control among boys were Internet Addiction, Internet Attitude and Protecting dimension of Parent Child Relationship. These variables are positively correlated which shows that they negatively influenced Loss of Behavioral/Emotional control among boys. Surprisingly, perceived overprotective parenting is also one of the significant predictor.

In case of girls the most significant predictors of Loss of Behavioral/Emotional Control was Internet Addiction only.

5.4.1d General Positive Affect

The result of stepwise regression analysis of Internet Communication and Parent-Child Relationship as Predictors of General Positive Affect among adolescent boys and girls is presented in Table 5.10 and Table 5.11, respectively.

Table 5.10: Stepwise Regression Analysis of Internet Communication and Parent- Child Relationship as Predictors of General Positive Affect among Adolescent Boys

Independent Variable	r	Beta Coefficient	t	R^2	R^2Change	F- Value (R^2 Change)
Protecting	-.399**	-.405	6.967**	.164	.164	48.544**
Internet Addiction	-.366**	-.219	3.247**	.198	.034	10.543**
Internet Usage	-.083	-.139	2.019**	.211	.013	4.076**

**p<.01; *p<.05

As it is evident from Table 5.10 that the significant predictor variables of General Positive Affect among the adolescent boys was Protecting dimension of Parent-Child Relationship (β =-.405, t = 6.967, p <.01), Internet Addiction (β =-.219, t = 3.247, p <.01), and Internet Usage (β =.139, t = 2.019, p <.01).

Thus, the lower General Positive Affect among boys was predicted by higher perception of mother's Protection, higher Internet Addiction and higher Internet Usage. These three variables accounted for 21.1 per cent of variance in the General Positive Affect of the adolescent boys. Out of this, the Protecting dimension of Parent-Child Relationship explained 16.4 per cent (F= 48.544, p< .01) of the variance, Internet Addiction explained an additional 3.4 per cent (F = 10.543, P<.01), and Internet Usage explained 1.3 per cent (F = 4.076, P<.01) of the variance in the General Positive Affect of the adolescent boys.

Table 5.11: Stepwise Regression Analysis of Internet Communication and Parent- Child Relationship as Predictors of General Positive Affect among Adolescent Girls

Independent variable	r	Beta Coefficient	t	R^2	R^2Change	F - Value (R^2 Change)
Internet Addiction	-.293**	-.587	11.420**	.345	.345	130.414**

**p<.01 and *p<.05

Table 5.11 reveals that the most significant predictor variable of General Positive Affect among adolescent girls came out to be Internet Addiction (β =-.587, t = 11.420, p <.01).Thus, it can be stated that as the Internet Addiction among girls increases it lowerstheir General Positive Affect. The variable accounted for a total of 34.5 per cent of variance in General Positive Affect (F= 130.414, P<.01).

Thus, it is evident from the above mentioned results that Internet Addiction has emerged to be the significant predictor of General Positive Affect among both boys and girls indicating that addiction to internet adversely effect the positive emotions among the selected students. Surprisingly,Protecting dimension of Parent-Child Relationship has emerged to be the most significant predictor of General Positive Affect among girls taking the major chunk of the variance but exerting a negative impact on the positive affect among girls.

5.4.1e Emotional Ties

The result of stepwise regression analysis of Internet Communication and Parent-Child Relationship as Predictors of Emotional Ties among adolescent boys and girls is presented in Table 5.12 and Table 5.13, respectively.

Table 5.12: Stepwise Regression Analysis of Internet Communication and Parent- Child Relationship as Predictors of Emotional Ties among Adolescent Boys

Independent Variable	r	Beta Coefficient	t	R^2	R^2Change	F- Value (R^2 Change)
Internet Attitude	-.275**	-.273	4.476**	.075	.075	20.033**
Internet Addiction	-.262**	-.239	2.771**	.141	.027	7.677**
Protection	-.226**	-.147	2.331**	.095	.020	5.431**
Internet Usage	.020	.149	2.345**	.114	.020	5.497**
Object Punishment	.090	.118	1.997**	.150	.014	3.987**

**p<.01; *p<.05

Table 5.12 reveals that the significant predictors of Emotional Ties among the adolescent boys were Internet Attitude (β = -.273, t = 4.476, p <.01), Internet Addiction (β =-.239, t = 2.771, p <.01) Protection (β =-.147, t = 2.331, p <.01), Internet Usage (β =.149, t = 2.345, p <.01) and Object Punishment (β =.118, t = 1.997, p <.01).

Thus, poor Emotional Ties among boys was predicted by higher Internet Attitude, Internet Addiction and perceived Protecting dimension of Parent-Child Relationship and positively correlated with Internet Usage and Object Punishment. These five variables were accounted for 15 per cent of variance in the Emotional Ties of the adolescent boys. Out of this, the Internet Attitude explained 7.5 per cent (F= 20.033, p< .01) of the variance,Internet Addiction explained 2.7 per cent (F =7.677, P<.01)Protecting explained an additional 2 per cent (F = 5.431, P<.01), Internet Usage took out 2 per cent (F = 9.425, P<.01)andObject Punishment accounted for 1.4 per cent (F = 3.987, P<.01)of the variance in the Emotional Ties of the adolescent boys.

Table 5.13: Stepwise Regression Analysis of Internet Communication and Parent-Child Relationship as Predictors of Emotional Ties among Adolescent Girls

Independent variable	r	Beta Coefficient	t	R^2	R^2Change	F -Value (R^2 Change)
Internet Addiction	-.266**	-.219	3.533**	.048	.048	12.481**
Internet Usage	.001	.173	2.557**	.072	.025	6.540**
Symbolic Reward	.124*	.123	2.020**	.088	.015	4.079**

**p<.01; *p<.05

As is evident from Table 5.13 the significant predictor variables of Emotional Ties among the adolescent girls was Internet Addiction (β = -.219, t = 3.533, p <.01), Internet Usage (β =-.147, t = 2.331, p <.01) and Symbolic Reward (β = .123, t = 2.020, p <.01).

Thus, above mentioned results shows that the poor Emotional Ties among girls was predicted by higher Internet Addiction but was positively correlated with Internet Usage and Symbolic Reward. These three variables accounted for 8.8 per cent of variance in the Emotional Ties of the adolescent girls. Out of this, Internet Addiction explained 4.8 per cent (F= 12.481, p< .01) of the variance, Internet Usage explained an additional 2.5 per cent (F = 6.540, P<.01) and Symbolic Reward accounted for 1.5 per cent (F = 4.079, P<.01)of the variance in the Emotional Ties of the adolescent girls.

It is noteworthy, that the most significant predictors of Emotional Ties emerged out to be Internet Attitude, Protection, Internet Usage, Internet Addiction and Object Punishment in which Internet Attitude, perceived Protecting dimension of Parent Child- Relationship and Internet Addiction have a negative impact on Emotional Ties whereas, Internet Usage and Object Punishment is positively correlated with Emotional Ties among boys.

In case of girls the most significant predictor of Emotional Ties was Internet Addiction which has a negative impact on emotional aspects, but contrary to this Internet Usage and Symbolic Reward are positively correlated with Emotional Ties among them.

5.4.1f Life Satisfaction

The result of stepwise regression analysis of Internet Communication and Parent-Child Relationship as Predictors of Life Satisfaction among adolescent boys and girls is presented in Table 5.14 and Table 5.15, respectively.

Table 5.14: Stepwise Regression Analysis of Internet Communication and Parent- Child Relationship as Predictors of Life Satisfaction among Adolescent Boys

Independent Variable	r	Beta Coefficient	t	R^2	R^2Change	F -Value (R^2 Change)
Protecting	-.371**	-.456	8.064**	.208	.208	65.034**
Internet Addiction	-.282**	-.269	4.148**	.259	.052	17.208**
Internet Usage	.009	.172	2.599**	.279	.020	6.753**
Neglecting	.067	.113	2.102**	.292	.013	4.416**

**p<.01; *p<.05

Table 5.13 reveals that the significant predictor variables of Life Satisfaction among the adolescent boys was Protecting (β = -.371, t = 8.064, p <.01), Internet Addiction (β =-.269, t = 4.148, p <.01), Internet Usage (β =.172, t = 2.599, p <.01) and Neglecting (β =.113, t = 2.102, p <.01).

Thus, the poor Life Satisfaction among boys was predicted by higher Protecting dimension of Parent-Child Relationship and Internet Addiction whereas, Internet Usage and surprisingly, Neglecting dimension of Parent-Child Relationship was having a positive correlation with Life Satisfaction among boys. These four variables accounted for 29.2 per cent of variance in the Life Satisfaction of the adolescent boys. Out of this, the Protecting explained 20.8 per cent (F= 65.034, p< .01) of the variance, Internet Addiction explained an additional 5.2 per cent (F = 17.208, P<.01), Internet Usage took out 2 per cent (F = 6.753, P<.01) and Neglecting accounted for 1.3 per cent (F = 4.416, P<.01)of the variance in the Life Satisfaction of the adolescent boys.

Table 5.15: Stepwise Regression Analysis of Internet Communication and Parent-Child Relationship as Predictors of Life Satisfaction among Adolescent Girls

Independent variable	r	Beta Coefficient	t	R^2	R^2Change	F - Value (R^2 Change)
Internet Addiction	-.360[**]	-.459	8.126**	.210	.210	66.024**
Internet Usage	.005	.204	3.343**	.244	.034	11.179**

**p<.01; *p<.05

Table 5.15 reveals that the significant predictor variables of Life Satisfaction among the adolescent girls were Internet Addiction (β = -.459, t = 8.126, p <.01), and Internet Usage (β = .204, t = 3.343, p <.01).

Thus, the poor life satisfaction among girls was predicted by higher Internet Addiction. Internet Usage was positively correlated with Life Satisfaction among them. These two variables accounted for 24.4 per cent of variance in the Life Satisfaction of the adolescent girls. Out of this, the Internet Addiction explained 21 per cent (F= 66.024, p< .01) of the variance, and Internet Usage explained an additional 3.4 per cent (F = 11.179, P<.01) of the variance in the Life Satisfaction of the adolescent girls.

Therefore, it is obvious from above results that the significant predictors of Life Satisfaction among adolescent boys were Protecting, Internet Addiction, Internet Usage and

Neglecting. More protecting approach perceived by the boys and higher Internet Addiction leads to poor Life Satisfaction and surprisingly, higher Internet Usage and perceived Neglecting dimension of Parent-Child Relationship leads to better Life Satisfaction among boys.

In case of girls, the most significant predictor emerged was Internet Addiction which has a negative impact on Life Satisfaction and at the same time Internet usage have a positive impact on Life Satisfaction among adolescent girls.

5.4.2 Stepwise Multiple Regression Analysis of Internet Communication and Parent-Child Relationship as Predictors of Psychosocial Adjustment among Boys and Girls

5.4.2a Emotional Adjustment

The result of stepwise regression analysis of Internet Communication and Parent-Child Relationship as Predictors of Emotional Adjustment among adolescent boys and girls is presented in Table 5.16 and Table 5.17, respectively

Table 5.16: Stepwise Regression Analysis of Internet Communication and Parent-Child Relationship as Predictors of Emotional Adjustment among Adolescent Boys

Independent Variable	r	Beta Coefficient	t	R^2	R^2 Change	F -Value (R^2 Change)
Internet Addiction	.424**	.424	7.369**	.180	.180	54.298**
Protecting	.476**	.257	3.870**	.227	.047	14.979**
Internet Attitude	.493**	.141	2.449**	.243	.016	5.259**
Internet Usage	.507**	-.146	2.161**	.257	.014	4.672**

**p<.01;*p<.05

As is evident from Table 5.16 that the significant predictor variables of Emotional Adjustment among the adolescent boys was Internet Addiction (β = .424, t = 7.369, p <.01), Protecting (β =.257, t = 3.870, p <.01), Internet Attitude (β =-.141, t = 2.449, p <.01) and Internet Usage(β =-.146, t = 2.161, p <.01).

Thus, the poor Emotional Adjustment among boys was predicted by higher Internet Addiction, Protecting, Internet Attitude and Internet Usage. These four variables accounted for 25.7 per cent of variance in the Emotional Adjustment of the adolescent boys. Out of this, the Internet Addiction explained 18 per cent (F= 54.298, p< .01) of the variance, Protecting explained an additional 4.7 per cent (F = 14.979, P<.01), Internet Attitude 1.6 per cent (F = 5.259, P<.01) and Internet Usage accounted for 1.4 per cent (F = 4.672, P<.01)of the variance in the Emotional Adjustment of the adolescent boys. Above mentioned results shows that these variables are having a negative impact on the Emotional Adjustment of boys.

Table 5.17: Stepwise Regression Analysis of Internet Communication and Parent-Child Relationship as Predictors of Emotional Adjustment among Adolescent Girls

Independent variable	r	Beta Coefficient	t	R^2	R^2 Change	F- Value (R^2 Change)
Internet Addiction	.342**	.342	5.733**	.117	.117	32.867**
Demanding	.366	.129	2.181**	.134	.017	4.756**
Indifferent	.385	-.122	2.071**	.149	.015	4.291**

**p<.01; *p<.05

Table 5.17 reveals that the significant predictor variables of Emotional Adjustment among the adolescent girls were Internet Addiction (β = .342, t = 5.733, p <.01), and demanding (β = .129, t = 2.181, p <.01).

Thus, higher Internet Addiction, Demanding and Indifferent dimension of Parent-Child Relationship leads to poor Emotional Adjustment among girls. These three variables accounted for 14.9 per cent of variance in the Emotional Adjustment of the adolescent girls. Out of this, the Internet Addiction explained 11.7 per cent (F= 32.867, p< .01) of the variance, and demanding explained an additional 1.7 per cent (F = 4.756, P<.01) and Indifferent account for total 1.5 per cent F = 4.291, P<.01) of the variance in the Emotional Adjustment of the adolescent girls.

It is noteworthy; from the above results that the most significant predictor emerged for poor Emotional adjustment among boys were higher Internet Addiction, Protecting dimension of

Parent Child Relationship, Internet Attitude and Internet Usage. Again perceived protecting approaches of mother's have a huge impact on the emotional adjustment of the boys.

5.4.2b Family Adjustment

The result of stepwise regression analysis of Internet Communication and Parent-Child Relationship as Predictors of Family Adjustment among adolescent boys and girls is presented in Table 5.18 and Table 5.19, respectively.

Table 5.18: Stepwise Regression Analysis of Internet Communication and Parent-Child Relationship as Predictors of Family Adjustment among Adolescent Boys

Independent Variable	r	Beta Coefficient	t	R^2	R^2Change	F- Value (R^2 Change)
Internet Addiction	-.317**	-.317	5.267**	.101	.101	27.742**
Protecting	-.067	.145	2.045**	.116	.015	4.182**

**p<.01;*p<.05

As is evident from Table 5.18 that the significant predictor variables of Family Adjustment among the adolescent boys was Internet Addiction (β = -.317, t = 5.267, p <.01) and Protecting(β =.145, t = 2.045, p <.01).

Surprisingly, the better Family Adjustment among boys was predicted by higher Internet Addiction and Protecting dimension of Parent Child Relationship. These two variables were accounted for 11.6 per cent of variance in the Family Adjustment of the adolescent boys. Out of this, the Internet Addiction explained 10.1 per cent (F= 27.742, p< .01) of the variance and Protecting explained an additional 1.5 per cent (F = 4.182, P<.01).

Table 5.19: Stepwise Regression Analysis of Internet Communication and Parent-Child Relationship as Predictors of Family Adjustment among Adolescent Girls

Independent variable	r	Beta Coefficient	t	R^2	R^2Change	F - Value (R^2 Change)
Internet Addiction	-.309**	-.309	5.122**	.096	.096	26.233**
Rejection	-.189**	-.177	2.966**	.127	.031	8.797**

| Object Punishment | -.173** | -.151 | 2.554** | .149 | .023 | 6.525** |

**p<.01; *p<.05

As is evident from Table 5.19 that the significant predictor variables of Family Adjustment among the adolescent girls was Internet Addiction (β = -.309, t = 5.122, p <.01), Rejection (β = -.177, t = 2.966, p <.01) and Object Punishment (β = -.151, t = 2.554, p <.01).

Thus, the better Family Adjustment among girls was predicted by higher Internet Addiction, Rejection and Object Punishment dimensions of Parent Child Relationship. These three variables were accounted for 14.9 per cent of variance in the Family Adjustment of the adolescent girls. Out of this, the Internet Addiction explained 9.6 per cent (F= 26.233, p< .01) of the variance, Rejection explained an additional 3.1 per cent (F = 8.797, P<.01), and Object Punishment accounted for 2.3 per cent (F = 6.525, P<.01)of the variance in the Family Adjustment of the adolescent girls.

As it is evident from the above results that the most significant predictor emerged for better Family adjustments among adolescent boys were Internet Addiction and Protecting dimension of Parent Child Relationship. These two variables had a positive impact on the family adjustment. In case of girls the most significant predictor was Internet Addiction, Rejection and Object Punishmentdimensions of Parent Child Relationship. Surprisingly, these three variables had a positive impact on the family adjustment among girls.

5.4.2c Health Adjustment

The result of stepwise regression analysis of Internet Communication and Parent-Child Relationship as Predictors of Health Adjustment among adolescent boys and girls is presented in Table 5.20 and Table 5.21, respectively

Table 5.20: Stepwise Regression Analysis of Internet Communication and Parent-Child Relationship as Predictors of Health Adjustment among Adolescent Boys

Independent Variable	r	Beta Coefficient	t	R^2	R^2Change	F-Value (R^2 Change)
Internet Addiction	.652**	.652	13.551**	.425	.425	183.642**

**p<.01; *p<.05

Table 5.20 reveals that the most significant predictor variable of Health Adjustment among the adolescent boys came out to be Internet Addiction (β =.652, t = 13.551, p <.01) .Thus it can be stated that higher Internet Addiction among boys decreases the Health Adjustment. The variable account for total 42.5 per cent of variance in Health Adjustment (F= 183.642, P<.01).

Table 5.21: Stepwise Regression Analysis of Internet Communication and Parent-Child Relationship as Predictor of Health Adjustment among Adolescent Girls.

Independent variable	r	Beta Coefficient	t	R^2	R^2Change	F-Value (R^2 Change)
Internet Addiction	.544**	.544	10.209**	.296	.296	104.224**

**p<.01; *p<.05

As is evident from Table 5.21 that the most significant predictor variable of Health Adjustment among the adolescent girls came out to be Internet Addiction (β =.544,t = 10.209, p <.01). As high scores shows poor adjustment it can be stated that the Internet Addiction among girls leads to the poor Health Adjustment. The variable account for total 29.6 per cent of variance in Health Adjustment (F= 104.224, P<.01).

It is noteworthy that the significant predictor of Health Adjustment emerged out to be Internet Addiction among both boys and girls, respectively. The above mentioned results show that the Internet Addiction has a bad impact on the Health adjustment among both the genders.

5.4.2d Social Adjustment

The result of stepwise regression analysis of Internet Communication and Parent-Child Relationship as Predictors of Social Adjustment among adolescent boys and girls is presented in Table 5.22 and Table 5.23, respectively

Table 5.22: Stepwise Regression Analysis of Internet Communication and Parent-Child Relationship as Predictors of Social Adjustment among Adolescent Boys

Independent Variable	r	Beta Coefficient	t	R^2	R^2Change	F- Value (R^2 Change)
Internet Addiction	.735**	.735	17.047**	.540	.540	290.601**

| Protecting | .580** | .261 | 5.384** | .588 | .048 | 28.984** |

**p<.01; *p<.05

As is evident from Table 5.22 that the most significant predictor variables of Social Adjustment among the adolescent boys came out to be Internet Addiction (β =.735, t = 17.047, p <.01) and Protecting (β =.261, t= 5.384, p <.01). As high scores shows poor adjustment, Thus, it can be stated that higher Internet Addiction and perceived Protecting dimension of Parent-Child Relationship among boys leads to poor Social Adjustment. The variable account for total 58.8 per cent of variance in Health Adjustment in which Internet Addiction account for (F= 290.601, P<.01) and Protecting explained (F= 28.984, P<.01) among adolescent boys.

Table 5.23: **Stepwise Regression Analysis of Internet Communication and Parent-Child Relationship as Predictors of Social Adjustment among Adolescent Girls**

Independent variable	r	Beta Coefficient	t	R^2	R^{2}Change	F- Value (R^2 Change)
Internet Addiction	.524**	.524	9.696**	.275	.275	94.014**

**p<.01; *p<.05

Table 5.23 reveals that the most significant predictor variable of Social Adjustment among the adolescent girls came out to be Internet Addiction (β = .524, t = 9.696, p <.01) .as high scores shows poor adjustment, Thus,it can be stated that as the Internet Addiction among girls increases the Social Adjustment among them decreases. The variable account for total 27.5 per cent of variance in Social Adjustment (F= 94.014, P<.01).

Therefore, it is obvious from above results that the significant predictors of poor Social Adjustment among adolescent boys were Internet Addiction and Protecting dimension of Parent Child Relationship. It may be because Perceived over protectiveness, restrictions, rearrangements in the home, and impairments in component skills contributes to poor social adjustment among boys.

In case of girls the most significant predictor emerged of Social Adjustment was Internet Addiction, which has a negative impact on Social Adjustment among them.

5.4.2e School Adjustment

The result of stepwise regression analysis of Internet Communication and Parent-Child Relationship as Predictors of School Adjustment among adolescent boys is presented in Table 5.24.

Table 5.24: Stepwise Regression Analysis of Internet Communication and Parent-Child Relationship as Predictors of School Adjustment among Adolescent Boys

Independent Variable	r	Beta Coefficient	t	R^2	R^2 Change	F - Value (R^2 Change)
Object Reward	-.136*	.-136	2.164**	.019	.019	4.685**

**p<.01; *p<.05

Table 5.24 reveals that the most significant predictor variable of School Adjustment among the adolescent boys came out to be Object Reward (β =.-136, t = 2.164, p <.01). As low scores shows better adjustment, thus, it can be stated that as the Object Reward among boys increases the School Adjustment among them .The variable account for total 1.9 per cent of variance in School Adjustment (F= 4.685, P<.01).

Thus, the most significant predictor of School adjustment was Object Reward among adolescent boys which show the positive impact on school adjustment. It may be because extending a reward to the child or a student helps to promote positive and appropriate behavior among them.

On the contrary, among the girls none of the variables emerged to be significant predictor of SchoolAdjustment.

5.4.3 Stepwise Multiple Regression Analysis of Internet Communication and Parent-Child Relationship Academic Performanceamong Boys and Girls

5.4.3.a Academic Performance (Boys)

The result of stepwise regression analysis of Internet Communication and Parent-Child Relationship as Predictors of Academic Performance among adolescent boys and girls is presented in Table 5.25 and Table 5.26, respectively.

Table 5.25: Stepwise Regression Analysis of Internet Communication and Parent-Child Relationship as Predictors of Academic Performance among Adolescent Boys

Independent Variable	r	Beta Coefficient	t	R^2	R^2 Change	F- Value (R^2 Change)
Internet Addiction	-.338**	-.338	5.664**	.115	.115	32.084**
Rejection	.192**	.169	2.869**	.143	.029	8.231**
Internet Usage	-.091	.163	2.290**	.161	.020	6.066**
Indifferent	.146*	.136	2.359**	.181	.018	5.565**
Symbolic Reward	.120	.143	2.463**	.200	.018	5.244**

**p<.01; *p<.05

5.4.3.b Academic Performance (Girls)

As is evident from Table 5.25 that the significant predictor variables of Academic Performance among the adolescent boys was Internet Addiction (β = -.338, t = 5.664, p <.01), Rejection (β = .169, t = 2.869, p <.01), Internet Usage (β = .163, t = 2.290, p <.01), Indifferent (β = .136, t = 2.359, p <.01) and Symbolic Reward (β = .143, t = 2.463, p <.01)

Thus, the poor Academic Performance among boys was predicted by higher Internet Addiction and Internet Usage. Rejection, Indifferent and Symbolic Reward dimensions of Parent-Child Relationship has a positive effect on Academic Performance among boys. These five variables were accounted for 20 per cent of variance in the Academic Performance of the adolescent boys. Out of this, the Internet Addiction explained 11.5 per cent (F= 32.084, p< .01) of the variance, Rejection explained an additional 2.9 per cent (F = 8.231, P<.01), Internet Usage took out 2 per cent (F = 6.066, P<.01), Indifferent accounted for 1.8 per cent (F = 5.265, P<.01) and Symbolic Reward took out for 1.8 per cent (F = 5.244, P<.01) of the variance in the Academic Performance of the adolescent boys.

Table 5.26: **Stepwise Regression Analysis of Internet Communication and Parent-Child Relationship as Predictors of Academic Performance among Adolescent Girls**

Independent variable	r	Beta Coefficient	t	R^2	R^2Change	F- Value (R^2 Change)
Internet Addiction	-.371**	-.371	6.295**	.138	.138	39.631**

**p<.01; *p<.05

As is evident from Table 5.26that the most significant predictor variable ofpoor Academic Performance among the adolescent girls came out to be Internet Addiction (β = -.371 t = 6.295, p <.01).Thus it can be stated that as the Internet Addictionincreases among girls the Academic Performance among them decreases. The variable account for total 2.1 per cent of variance in Academic Performance (F= 39.631, P<.01).

In sum, the above results indicated that Academic Performance in terms of Internet Addiction and Internet Usage have significant and negative effect on Academic Performance among boys and Rejection, Indifferent and symbolic reward have a significant and positive impact on Academic Performance among boys, which indicates that as the above mentioned perceived Parent-Child Relationship dimensions increases the Academic Performance among boys also increases. In case of girls, the only significant predictor of poor Academic Performance was Internet Addiction.

Thus, it is obvious from the above results that the significant predictor of Academic Performance among both boys and girls was Internet Addiction and this variable negatively influenced the Academic Performance among them. Surprisingly, in case of boys Rejection and Indifferent dimensions of Parent-Child Relationship have a positive impact on Academic Performance.

CPSIA information can be obtained
at www.ICGtesting.com
Printed in the USA
BVHW031413060922
646321BV00013B/477